Advance praise for
CROOKED TEETH

"I take my hat off to Danny Ramadan and his brilliant muses. This is a mesmerizing story of growing up gay in a Muslim Syrian family, of the challenges and joys of finding and creating loving communities, and the miracle not just of physical survival but of an effervescent celebration of the human heart. Once I began reading, I couldn't stop until the final page. Countless others will be thankful for this raw, idiosyncratic, utterly compelling account of Danny's long journey home." —Lawrence Hill, author of *The Illegal*

"Danny Ramadan's vigorous prose is poised in that enchanted place between master storytelling and testimonial. Written with the skill of a fiction writer, *Crooked Teeth* is sweeping and intimate, a memoir of bloody revolution and bear hugs. Danny Ramadan asks if he can trust us with his story. Discover what trust means. Read this book." —Kim Echlin, author of *Speak, Silence*

"*Crooked Teeth* is a tender invitation into the life and mind of one of Canada's favourite and most acclaimed authors. Here is a memoir that coaxes as it resists, all through Ramadan's familiar, luscious, and generative literary voice. First-time readers will no doubt be inspired by his bravery, nimble storytelling, and deft application of craft. Fans of his other work will recognize this book as the homecoming it truly is." —Jenny Heijun Wills, author of *Older Sister. Not Necessarily Related.*

CROOKED TEETH

A Queer Syrian
Refugee Memoir

DANNY
RAMADAN

VIKING

VIKING

an imprint of Penguin Canada, a division of Penguin Random House Canada Limited

Canada • USA • UK • Ireland • Australia • New Zealand • India • South Africa • China

First published 2024

www.penguinrandomhouse.ca

LIBRARY AND ARCHIVES CANADA CATALOGUING IN PUBLICATION

Title: Crooked teeth : a queer Syrian refugee memoir / Danny Ramadan.
Names: Ramadan, Ahmad Danny, author.
Identifiers: Canadiana (print) 20230561586 | Canadiana (ebook) 20230561675 |
    ISBN 9780735242210 (softcover) | ISBN 9780735242227 (EPUB)
Subjects: LCSH: Ramadan, Ahmad Danny. | LCSH: Novelists, Canadian—
    21st century—Biography. | LCSH: Refugees—Syria—Biography. |
    LCSH: Refugees—Canada—Biography. | LCSH: Sexual minorities—
    Biography. | CSH: Authors, Canadian (English)—21st century—Biography. |
    LCGFT: Autobiographies.
Classification: LCC PS8635.A4613 Z46 2024 | DDC C813/.6—dc23

Cover and interior design by Jennifer Griffiths
Typeset by Sean Tai
Cover images: (bulldozer) © andrewburgess / Adobe Stock Images

Printed in Canada

10 9 8 7 6 5 4 3 2

Penguin
Random House
VIKING CANADA

To Matthew

I am in a swimming pool.

You emerge, take a deep breath, and smile. You carry me on your back to the shallow end. I wrap my arms and legs around you and laugh like a child, my cheek warm on your shoulder.

You whisper that you love me.

Everything shines.

What happens is most people get older. They honor their credit cards, they find parking spaces, they marry . . . But to grow up costs the earth . . . It means you take responsibility for the time you take up . . . You find out what it costs us to love and to lose, to dare and to fail. And maybe even more, to succeed. What it costs, in truth . . . That's what I write . . . I'm just telling a very simple story.
MAYA ANGELOU

A home is not necessarily a large land. It could be as small as the space between two shoulders.
GHASSAN KANAFANI

DISCLAIMER

Memories are faulty by nature, and traumatized brains tend to create narratives of sorrow to justify the hurt. Describing an incident that happened years before depends on the creative and the assumptive, even when it aims at telling the truth.

Some names are changed to respect people I couldn't ask for permission.

CROOKED TEETH

TRUST

Writing this memoir is a betrayal.

It feels like a toppling of every wall I've ever built, like poking holes in the layers of protection I stretched around my wounds like bubble wrap. It feels like a disloyalty to my fiction, which has served as my shield for two decades now. Writing fiction is much safer, and it's better for my mental health. I know where to cut deep and where to tread softly. I know where to merge my truth into the realm of the story. I am skilled in the fictional hide and seek. I slip myself between my lines and on the margins. I pull the white of the page over my body like bedding and sleep there, comfortable that no one will find me.

But where to hide in the pages of a memoir? How to escape when the words are my face, the ink is my blood, the paper is my skin?

If I am to map my truth on these pages, am I not revealing my tricks to my readers like an amateur magician? Will you return to my novels and sniff me out from between the pages, interrupting the slumber of my hurt there?

Matthew, my husband, tells me that writing this memoir is a gift. That I can offer an authentic representation of the queer refugee experience and build a genuine understanding of the intricate details of my story. He says that I can write it with agency, reflecting not just on my trauma but also on my resilience.

I resist. My resilience is not a single-use item that I acquired. I'm in a constant state of mending. I catch and release my triggers and traumas like an ethical fisherman, returning them to the sea of my soul. I search in my day-to-day life for a moment of peace that I hold on to like a candle in a cave. On days like today, my story of resilience feels fragile and breakable. Other days it brings me comfort, lulling me with the fruits of my labour: the healthy body I live in, the supportive husband I have, the beautiful home I own. My writing. My community of lovers and friends.

Like a peaceful warrior I endured, and I came out victorious. Scars on my back and broken ribs, chin up high and eyes glittering with pride. Wounds to be stitched, triumphs to be celebrated.

How would I ensure that this complex narrative of my experience is held tenderly by every reader? How would I offer you my queer trauma on these pages if I can't trust you to hold space for my Syrian pride as well, for my Canadian success? Where will you weigh in on the balance between empathy and sympathy? Will you tear up when I tell you about my lows? Will you find me cocky when I celebrate my highs? Did you pick up this memoir with an expectation based on your preconceived notion of what a refugee is, what a gay man is, what a Syrian is? Are you willing to let go of these notions at the turn of this page and trust me in the telling of my own story? Are you willing to let go of the simple narrative of here is "good" and there is "bad" when it comes to refugees arriving in Canada? Will you trust me, as I am about to trust you?

Typing every word on these pages is my own act of trusting you, and trusting you with my truth goes against every defence mechanism I have acquired throughout my life.

⬤

Here is why it is difficult to trust you:

I once struck up a conversation with a woman on an airplane. I'd spent a long weekend in Ottawa as part of the International Writers Festival, following the release of my debut novel, and was on my way back to Vancouver. She was on her way to White Rock to visit her sister, who'd just had a baby. We started with small talk, comparing the icy October winds of Ottawa with the rainy days of Vancouver, commenting on the lack of legroom between seats and the man in front of us who'd dropped his seatback all the way down, practically resting his head in my lap. *(Seriously? On a daytime flight?)* She offered me a mandarin orange, and I offered her the name of the fruit in Arabic.

"Yousef Afandi," I enunciated.

"Isn't Yousef the name of a person?" she asked.

"Yeah, it's the Arabic equivalent of Joseph. Afandi also means mister or boss, so the name of the fruit is Mr. Yousef."

"Huh." She slipped another slice between her lips. "Why name a fruit after a person?"

"I honestly don't know."

We both chuckled, then she pulled out her phone to show me pictures of her newborn niece and I pulled out my novel from my backpack, proudly presenting it to her.

"What's it about?" She examined the back cover, the author photo with my dyed red hair, then flipped through the pages of the book. She landed on the front cover again, adorned with stamps of approval by awards juries and best-of lists.

"It's a story of two gay refugees leaving Syria and arriving in Canada, then reflecting on their journey as they build a home for themselves in Vancouver."

"Oh, so it's a memoir."

"No," I said. "It's a novel."

She leafed through the book and asked if she could read from it. I nodded and watched her fold the book to its first page, cracking the spine.

I'd never watched anyone read my own work in real time. I tried to busy myself with my gadgets, playing a sitcom on my iPad. But between laugh tracks I heard her gasp. She licked her index finger and turned the page. She held in her hands my author's copy—a sacred book with my own highlights, corrections for future editions, and Post-it notes with scribbled Arabic and English words. My notes in the margins haunted me. *What have I done?*

Eventually she turned to me, and I pulled my headphones out of my ears. The first chapter is filled, almost to the brim, with loving scenes. It narrates the meet-cute of the two lovers, albeit against a backdrop of civil war and homophobia, but it was, at least in my opinion, an uplifting chapter.

"I am so sorry." Tears gathered in her eyes.

"For what?"

"I'm sorry this happened to you. That must have been horrible."

Where did she find me in that chapter? I'd hidden my face well under fictional characters and elaborate metaphors. Still, out of the joyful intimate scenes, the sweet coffees and warm embraces, she pulled out only Damascus. A version of the city, anyway. A version seen through a North American lens, of a city darkened by war, a country in a state of destruction, a man in an endless cycle of trauma. That version of Damascus is almost comical in its simplicity, borrowing images from pop culture and mainstream media—sandy deserts and post-apocalyptic landscapes, belly dancers and mobs of faceless refugees at sea. It contradicted everything I knew about my homeland.

Her tears felt like pity. I thought they were even rude. With each one I got smaller in her vision; I wasn't a man anymore. I descended into a creature of misfortune, a walking, talking charcoaled war victim. I fought the urge to snap the book out of her hand.

"Damascus was such a cruel place to you," she said. "I'm glad you're here now."

It's true that I'm a queer man who grew up in a homophobic society; Damascus force-fed me its cruelty on a daily basis. But it also spoke to me in my mother tongue and giggled at my jokes. It opened its arms and embraced me on a late-night stroll, and it hid me within its alleyways as I had my first kiss. It covered me with its star-dotted sky when I had no home but its roads.

Her tears wouldn't stop. She told me she'd never met a Syrian refugee before, but she'd followed the news of the civil war for years and had donated to a local church in Ottawa sponsoring a Syrian family. She asked if I knew them, failing in her attempt to pronounce the Arabic surname. Other passengers had started to look at us and a concerned flight attendant passed by, assessing the situation.

I moved into the empty seat between us, aware that people had begun to whisper, and put a comforting hand on her upper back. "The world is such a horrible place sometimes," she said. "I am so sorry for you."

"It's okay. I'm here now. I'm okay. I'm right here," I repeated until she calmed down. I didn't want to engage with her anymore, but I wanted this awkward situation to be over. I doubted she would listen if I were to attempt a genuine conversation about how limited her views were. Instead I joined in her fantasy and reassured her. The gay Syrian refugee was saved. Thank you, nameless airplane woman, for personally making it possible for me to live my best gay life. Yup, all saved right here. Canada is good that way. *O Canada, our home and native land*. All was well here, flight attendants, no need to call air marshals on the brown man who made a white woman cry.

Finally, she blew her nose into the airline napkin I handed her, cleared her throat, and looked out the window. I returned to my aisle seat and pretended to be asleep for the rest of the flight.

◠

But then, if I did not tell you this story, I'd leave the space for other— namely white—authors to tell it. I don't know what it is about the refugee experience that so inspires white authors to capture it in fiction and non-fiction. I can't tell you how many times I've sat in an audience watching yet another writer read from their acclaimed book, *giving a voice to the voiceless*, peppering their narrative with *inshallahs* and *yalla habibis*. The memoir by an author who went to Turkey for six months to volunteer at a refugee camp, which included a chapter about a refugee mother who was so thankful for his services that she named her baby after him. The famed author who wrote yet another novel set during a civil war he hadn't lived through, with limited understanding of the socio-political factors in such a war, not to mention the economic and religious tensions between his characters. The yoga instructor who wrote a book about her experience starting a GoFundMe to pay for a trip to Jordan to teach Syrian children yoga at a refugee camp, who couldn't handle my asking her, point-blank, whether the money she raised could have benefited these children in better ways, namely with food, shelter, and education.

Here I go, weighing in on the cultural appropriation debate. I can almost see the eye rolls. This is where I invite you to start practising that trust we discussed earlier.

I'm not actually against white authors depicting the refugee experience. I write female characters all the time despite having no claim over femininity. If I'm only to write characters I identify with, I'd have a very limited pool.

But I believe that the refugee voice deserves respect. Research needs to be done—deep dives into the geopolitical, economic, religious, and personal aspects of the refugee experience—along with a willingness to question the place this work would occupy.

And even despite thorough research and intense dedication, there are details that an outsider to a particular culture is bound to get wrong. In English, for example, when something makes you happy, you say that it warms your heart. In Upper Arabic, the language we write novels and read the news in, you say that it ices your chest. Think about it. English is a language born in a cold climate, where warmth brings memories of joyful summer days. Arabic is a language born in the middle of a desert, where a chill is what brings such bliss.

I would hope that authors who write about experiences outside their own are asking themselves whose seat at the table they're taking away. When they take up the space, it affects the way we as marginalized artists are viewed, read, interviewed, marketed, and valued.

Here, let me give you an example:

As part of my first Canadian book tour, I was invited to a high-end small-town writers' festival in a fancy resort hotel on the East Coast. I was offered a handsome amount of money and an extended stay at a hotel. Still agentless at the time, soft around the edges and eager to please, I accepted the invitation without paying attention to the details of the panels I was to be featured on. I flew across the country and stayed in the extravagant hotel, mesmerized by my room's view of the lake, its large workspace, and its deep bathtub.

Awaiting me on the bed was a package containing two pieces of decadent chocolate with the festival logo emblazoned on their wrappers, a fine-tip pen, an expensive notebook, my payment cheque, my name tag, an all-access lanyard, and the festival program.

Relaxed after a hot bath, I checked the program descriptions and found, to my surprise, that I'd been grouped with three non-fiction writers on a panel about seeking refuge. Was there a reason I was the sole novelist on this panel? I hadn't read any of the other authors before, but their bios were filled with accolades and honours.

The next evening I was introduced by the facilitator, a well-known radio personality, who mispronounced my name and then made a joke about it to the amusement of the attendees. I took the stage with a smile and sat, as instructed, in the farthest seat from him.

The event began when the rest of the panelists joined us onstage, lavished with applause. I felt a bit uncomfortable that I was the only non-white person in the group. I stood out like a rotten tooth. Whereas the other authors wore expensive suits and blingy watches, I had on a pair of runners and a T-shirt that showcased my sleeve of tattoos. It was clear that the facilitator knew some of them personally, and they conversed with enthusiasm. He asked them elaborate questions on the impact of the refugee crisis globally, the Canadian government's Syrian Refugee Resettlement program, the role refugees and new immigrants play in the financial future of an aging population, and more.

Slowly, I was forgotten. I slipped into the shadows at the end of the stage, nodding politely when one of them made a good point, laughing when one of their jokes landed. I questioned whether anyone at the festival had actually read my work or knew that my novel was not a memoir. Had I been invited based on my merit and my talent, or was I a brown face to be added to the otherwise white panel discussing refugees? Had I sold my identity for two pieces of chocolate and a hot bath?

It took the facilitator twenty-eight minutes of the one-hour panel to ask me my first question.

"Akhmed—" The *khh* sound, foreign to my birth name, almost burst my ear.

"I actually prefer if you call me Danny." I'd already told the organizers that although my official name is Ahmad, my preferred name is Danny.

"Danny." He laughed. "You're a newly arrived refugee. Did you feel welcomed when you came to Canada?"

My insides burned. If I hadn't paused before speaking, I think I would have breathed fire. "That's a trick question, don't you think?"

"Is it?"

"I think this kind of question really traps me in a corner," I said. "It leaves me with two options. I could say yes, I felt welcomed, which in turn simplifies my experience as a newcomer to this country facing unique challenges that neither myself nor the Canadian community accounted for before my arrival. Or I could say no, which would alienate the two hundred people in the audience who I hope will buy my book after this panel."

Silence fell on the crowd, then some of the attendees clapped in approval.

"I think you left all the juicy questions to these wonderful folks," I said, gesturing to the other panelists. I'd switched from my serious tone to a more mischievous one, breaking the awkwardness of the situation. The facilitator fake-laughed and asked if I had anything to add to the preceding conversation. I took the space with hunger: I elaborated on my criticism of the Canadian response to the refugee crisis, enumerated steps to include in the Private Sponsorship program to ensure equity and transparency between the refugees and the volunteer sponsors, and centred my experience in the conversation. The hour passed, and the line for me to sign books was longer than any other.

I was never invited back to that festival.

◖

I wish I could tell you that this was abnormal.

Instead, I could tell you about the time Reni Eddo-Lodge, author of *Why I'm No Longer Talking to White People About Race*, asked the facilitator of a panel to let me speak in response to a co-panelist's anti-immigration statements, and the facilitator told her they didn't have time.

I could tell you about the award-winning author who answered a question about her stance on refugees with "Of course we should take in more," and then, "Who else would clean our streets and take care of our elders?" while I sat in the front row beside a fellow brown author with an immigration background, our readings slated for right after hers.

It's maddening. Stories about queer people of colour are embraced when the narrative includes a white saviour, or when the closed-minded, homophobic society of birth makes Canada appear perfectly open and welcoming. In writing this memoir, I want to tell you that it's not as simple as that. Sometimes my approach might feel confrontational. I've long prided myself on being polite instead of quarrelsome, but some patterns are meant to be broken.

Writing this memoir also feels like wading barefoot into settled muddy water. After years of therapy, a blissful marriage, and a successful integration into the Canadian community, my traumas are hibernating crocodiles resting at the bottom of my swamp. Why would I disturb them? Maybe writing this memoir is worth it when I do it on my own terms, respecting my agency and honouring my voice. But then, what happens when this book is out in the world? For women on planes to read and weep over inconsolably? For panelists to skim and simplify? Will I still think it's worth it a year from now? Two years? Twenty?

Finally, can I rely on you to see my talent as a writer? Can I trust you to read the raw, honest, and sorrowful stories I share, but also see my art? I offer you my life story, but I also offer you my craft. My metaphors, a meld of two languages poured on the page like golden rims on glasses. My control of narrative, balancing the internal journey with the external incidents. Are you willing to suspend your disbelief when you read my dialogue in order to understand the truth beneath the words on the page? Will you accept my leaning on the tools of fiction to tell a story that's anything but?

I could go on, but I want to stop here and extend my hand to you. Together, let's come to an agreement on this memoir.

I promise you that I will tell you everything I know of myself, to the best of my ability, and try to frame that with my own understanding of the world I was born in, the world I was a refugee in, and the world I call home. I promise not to shy away from moments of hurt that I otherwise keep to myself and my therapist. I promise to put my fiction in a drawer and pull out my mirror instead. I will look at my past with as much of a critical eye as I can, and I will present you with my disappointments alongside my triumphs, my sorrow alongside my joy. I will revisit the moments I failed others while also attempting to understand those who failed me.

You, on the other hand, need to promise that you will trust me as I trust you. Promise that you will take what I write here, absorb it, and use it to question the notions you have about refugees, about Syrians, about queer men, about those who—like me—are all three. Promise that you will see not only my story but also my art. Promise that you will listen. That you'll hold space for my joy alongside my sorrow, my disappointments alongside my triumphs. That you'll forgive those I want to forgive.

I read somewhere that trauma changes you. It turns your mind upside down, shakes you to the core, and blinds you. As you'll see, my traumas brought out a side of me I dislike: cynical, unapproachable, and frightened by the world. Healing, however, changes you, too. Healing doesn't bring you back to the naive child you were before the trauma. It matures you into someone capable of caring for yourself and others. I am broken by the past, but I am thankful for its healing.

This is not an invitation for you to be a voyeur of the beautiful mess that is my life. It's an opportunity for you to examine your own life and how you lead it. I want you to challenge yourself, to broaden your horizons, to find your blind spots and colour them with my words.

I will unbutton my shirt and show my scars. But the story won't be complete unless you bare your own.

Otherwise, what's the point?

THEN

Some stories are better understood when you start from the beginning.

Even if you as a writer have an aversion to linear narratives.

MOTHER

They say that when your parents get a divorce, you end up with two of everything. Two bedrooms, two backpacks, two dinner tables, two birthdays. I ended up with none.

When I was seventeen, my parents' divorce loomed. Anyone who saw them together knew they wouldn't last the year. Neighbours whispered about the impending split; maiden aunts anticipated it. Local shop owners, from whom I regularly purchased meat and eggs, stopped allowing me to add to my father's tab and demanded an instant payment instead, leaving our fridge empty.

Sometimes I wouldn't see my father for weeks. He'd couch-surf at the homes of various friends and uncles or crash at the real estate office where he worked. If he didn't score a place to stay he'd drive around until he was positive my mother had gone to sleep, drugged with whatever medicine prescribed to her by the series of psychologists and herbalists she frequented.

On a rainy winter day, my mother had one of her bad episodes: She ran out onto our balcony with a large pot from the kitchen. Her hair was uncovered, her undergarments thin, wet, and revealing. She threw the pot through the neighbour's window, smashing the glass, and proudly stood there while the stunned woman shouted at her.

"You are a witch!" my mother shouted back. "You cursed my marriage!"

It took me half an hour to get her back inside. First I begged and pleaded, and then I cried. She wouldn't move. She hurled insults at our neighbour, who ignored her and retreated into her home. Ten minutes later her husband appeared at the window, surveying the scene of the crime.

Other neighbours from the slums we lived in watched on. Some hid behind curtains, and some didn't bother.

"Please come inside." I pulled on my mother's slippery arms. "Everyone is looking at us."

Her eyes were black like the night sky, unblinking. She was a statue firmly anchored to the ground. The rain gathered her chestnut hair in tangled clumps. "She wants to steal your father," she whispered. "She wants to burn our house down. We only have one home. Where else would we go? Where else would we go?"

Finally she gave in and allowed me to drag her inside. I grabbed a dirty towel from the mountain of laundry in the kitchen, dried her hair, and made her a cup of tea. She mumbled something about the song of fire she'd heard the neighbours recite. *They were calling the devil*, she insisted. *They worship the flame*, she protested. *They slaughter stray cats and eat them*, she whispered. I nodded, handed her a pill from her bedside table, and waited by her bed until she dozed off.

On the balcony, I watched our neighbour clean the broken glass.

"I am sorry, uncle!" I shouted. He used a wooden stick to smash the remaining glass stuck to the window frame.

"She is sick," I said.

He sighed loudly and broke more glass. "Tell your father to talk to me." He avoided eye contact.

We stood in silence while the remaining glass shattered with his repeated knocks. He caught some of it in a plastic bucket while other pieces slipped down the eight floors and plinked in the narrow alleyway below.

"There's no way to salvage this," he mumbled. "I need to break the whole window and replace it."

Over the next week I watched him outfit the frame with plastic bags before installing a new sheet of glass. His wife, the accused witch, no longer looked out the window. I kept an eye on my mother, worried that another assault might take place.

"Is your father back home yet?" the neighbour asked when he ran into me on the street.

"Maybe tonight."

As we waited for his return, I'd gotten into the habit of turning our living room into a dorm of sorts for me and my younger sisters, Nour and Lara: pillows assembled from our three beds, mismatched mattresses on the floor. I feared that my mother would attempt to harm one of us at night, so I gathered us to keep watch.

"We spend the nights here for warmth," I told them. They no longer asked their usual questions: Why is Mama angry? When will Baba be home?

"I need you to sign the school report, Ahmad," Nour said. I would forge my father's signature whenever needed. I nodded and listened to their giggles getting quieter until they finally fell asleep. I stayed up, mesmerized by the crackling fire.

Motherless daughters, I was taught growing up, were the fruit that fell off a tree too green. Who would teach them the ways of the woman's world? Who would show them the many roads they couldn't take, the endless list of forbidden thoughts and acts, if not their mother, who'd learned the same restrictions from her own? Our extended family understood that my sisters were as good as motherless daughters, that their chances of an honourable marriage with a desirable family were narrowing as the winter days shortened.

Was I to be their mother? I had been motherless longer than they had. Like a hot coal, I'd been tossed among the hands of tired grandmothers and young aunts. I was hastily returned to my mother's house with no guidance on how to turn her from the unstable person she was into the fantasy image of a mother I'd seen on television and in the homes of my schoolmates.

Around two o'clock in the morning my father opened the front door, walked into the living room, and stumbled upon our makeshift beds.

"You need to divorce her," I whispered, startling him.

"Why are you still up?"

"You need to divorce her, man." I sat up. My sisters mumbled in their sleep. "These girls are getting older. Who will raise them? I can't raise them!"

"Don't talk about something you don't understand," he stagewhispered, loud enough to emote anger, low enough to ensure my mother wouldn't wake.

"She's a lost cause." I stood up from my mattress. I'd grown over the past two years, shot up to my father's height. "Think of the girls."

He untied his shoes and pulled them off one after the other, revealing his holed socks. The room stank of his feet as he walked toward the fireplace to warm his hands by the smouldering fire.

"You owe our neighbour the price of a window."

His back stiffened. "I will talk to your grandmother." He took off his socks and sniffed them, scrunched his nose, then threw them by the fireplace. "Now go to sleep."

Let's do some math, why don't we?

My parents met in their first year of university, which is the point in the Syrian education system when gender-segregated schooling ends. My father studied to be an engineer, and my mother studied to be a biology teacher. Damascus University's School of Engineering and School of Biology are next to each other, separated by a side street. The school year in Syria, as in most of the world, starts in September. It stands to reason, then, that the earliest they could have met was September 1983.

"They are not cut from our cloth," my paternal grandmother made a point of telling me many times growing up, referring to her son's in-laws.

The two families were from different economic backgrounds. My father came from a working-class family with a well-known bloodline. The family tree, drawn on a large canvas with golden threads, was well-documented and hung ceremoniously in my grandparents' home. My uncles owned businesses or worked for the government. An aunt married into the rich family of a beloved Syrian actor.

My mother came from a poverty-stricken family. Her father owned a small kabab stand in the capital's chop-shop district, which he commuted to on his rusty bike, even in old age. None of the uncles or aunts on this side of the family finished school, with my mother being the first to attend university.

My parents' wedding night was in late October 1983, less than two months after the start of the school year. I was born seven months later, at the end of May 1984, and was claimed to be a child of a premature delivery. When I was born my father was nineteen and my mother was eighteen.

It is traditional for Damascene weddings to happen in late spring, away from the colder, wetter months of winter. Yet here my parents were, getting married in the coldest month of the year.

Whereas my mother is the eldest of her brothers and sisters, my father was the third in a line of brothers—fourth, if you count my uncle who died a soldier in the 1973 war with Israel. It's traditional in Syria, especially in Sunni working-class families like his, for the sons of the family to marry one after another, according to their order of birth. My father broke tradition: he was the first of his brothers to get married, years before his older brothers.

Syrian men are also expected to finish two and a half years of mandatory military service before getting married, yet my father wed before his began; my parents ended up spending the first three years of their marriage apart, as he was appointed to a brigade in a different city.

Their marriage was branded a union of love, a significant difference from the arranged marriages of all my uncles and aunts on both sides of the family. And yet anyone with eyes could tell that there was no love lost between my parents. The fact that it was society's disdain for divorce keeping them together wasn't simply speculation, it was stated as fact among extended family.

My sister Nour was born seven years after me, another deviation from the family tradition of producing children on an annual basis for the economic purpose of adding working hands to the household.

So, it stands to reason that I was a son of a sin. A bastard. A child conceived out of wedlock.

I have no proof of this. My mother did not sit me down and tell me an empowering feminist story of accepting her body and the fruit she bore. No grandmother with jasmine flowers hidden in her bra whispered wise words of love and sorrow in my young ears. No diary of a sinful woman was ever found in a forgotten box in an attic with faded photos of lovers.

I simply did the math.

My maternal grandmother said I was born with jaundice. "Your mother was so sad to see you suffer," she said. "Her chest couldn't produce milk to feed you."

She explained that my mother refused to celebrate the birth the way other women in Syria did. She did not welcome a gathering of women in her mother's home for a traditional tea and dessert, nor did she accept gifts from sisters and aunts wishing her well. She pushed for me to be cared for by her own mother while she rested and recuperated alone. My grandmother accepted the task, with the help of my two young aunts.

She passed me to the men of the family only once on the night of my birth. "They needed to pray in your ear," she told me. "To induct you into Islam."

Praying in a newborn's ear informs a child of their appointed religion. It usually falls on the father to recite the call to prayer, heard across Islamic countries five times a day. My father must have held me in one arm, lifted me up high in the middle of a room, then sung loudly into my ear before repeating the call in a lowered voice.

"You were so calm," my grandmother said. "Other children would fuss or cry, but you were born ready to take on the faith of Islam."

My grandmother hoped that my mother's breast milk would pour out with time, but she was disappointed when months passed and it did not. She took my mother to herbalists and offered her medicinal teas.

"Allah, You who melt iron, melt the milk in this chest for this child. We ask You to help this woman feed her baby. She is weak, and You are Mighty and Blessing." She recited Quranic prayers over her daughter's head while she slept. Nothing worked, and my grandmother had to rely completely on formula for my growing body.

In hindsight, the signs of postnatal depression were there: the disconnect from the child, the inability to produce milk, the isolation and despair. My mother surely would have benefited from a knowledgeable therapist or an understanding family.

After my birth, the pressure on her to drop out of college must have been enormous.

"I want to be a biology teacher," I picture her saying to her family, her curly hair bouncing as she argued. She often expressed this sentiment to me as time went on. "I wanted to finish my studies."

"You have no business going out to universities alongside random men," they must have told her. "Stay home and raise your child. That's what you were meant to do all along."

My father dropped out of college, too. He packed his bags, put on the military camouflage and the heavy boots, and went away for six months at a time. My mother, following tradition, quickly joined her new family, moving into her in-laws' centuries-old Damascene house—the first place I would ever call home.

●

Some have trouble imagining their parents as young people, but I never knew mine any other way. My mother was barely twenty when she moved in with her in-laws. When I was twenty I could scarcely take care of myself, let alone a growing child and a demanding household of strangers. My grandfather's house required an army of women to clean and maintain it. My father, often away in the military, was rarely able to give my mother a phone call or write her a letter. She was completely alone, disconnected from everything she knew and probably everything she hoped for or imagined for herself.

Were my father and mother ever in love? I remember only their dysfunctional dynamics and vicious fights. The echo of the slap he planted on her cheek. Her wet face narrowly avoiding the water glass he hurled at her. I don't remember the contents of the arguments, only their intensity: starting with whispers, then growing into louder exclamations, duelling monologues, and eventually guttural shouts. Then, after locking horns like mountain goats, they'd retreat to separate corners of the room, exchanging dirty looks, unsure of what to do next.

These arguments never resolved the issue at hand. It seemed to me as though the fighting was the purpose: to release such brawling energy into the wild, then sit satisfied with their empty chests.

"I think he wants to divorce her," I once told my maternal grandmother. I'd called her after one of their fights ended with my mother crying in a corner and my father storming out. During the fight he'd gutted the closet of her clothes, which he threw onto the bed; the mirror on the closet door had broken with his smack.

"That cannot be," my grandmother said. "Let me talk to her!"

"She doesn't want to come to the phone."

"You tell him, then," she demanded. "Find your father and beg him not to divorce your mother."

I must have been four.

My parents had to remain together, forced into their marriage by the one factor neither of them could overcome: the child they had together. Although divorce is legal in Syria and permitted in Islam, it's considered the worst of all fates for a woman, especially a mother. A divorced woman loses her value as she'd lost her virginity. Suitors would assume she was barren or difficult. Courters would ask why they should feed someone else's child. Divorced daughters return to their parents' home with very little chance of ever leaving it again, cowering in corners, serving life sentences at the lowest level of the Syrian family hierarchy, right below maiden aunts. They become an easier target for claims of promiscuity: without the stamp of confirmation that their virginity is intact, what would keep them from prowling the streets for evil men to satisfy their sexual desires? My community raised me to believe that a divorced woman is a woman of no moral guidance.

I sometimes wonder if my mother saw me as the reason for her misery. If it weren't for me she would have finished college, gotten a teaching job, maybe even fallen in love with a fellow teacher who didn't feel threatened by a working wife. She would have had agency in the path she found, the decisions she made, the future she built.

My mother hid a small notebook in her closet under layers of clothes.

The notebook was lined with song lyrics she liked and drawings she'd done of herself and others. I leafed through it a few times over the years, noticing it filling up with her art. I imagine her in her free time, away from the many chores and tasks a daughter-in-law was required to do, sneaking back to her bedroom, sitting on the lush Persian carpet, and flipping through the notebook or drawing a new face on its pages.

She spoke French as fluently as her limited Syrian education allowed and played songs by Édith Piaf and Dalida on a small boombox in our bedroom. I saw the lyrics to the songs in her notebook. Her handwriting was precious, minding her accents on the French words. She sometimes sang along, guided by her notebook. Hushing her voice so as not to be heard by the other women in the house, she'd act out the emotions of the singers, rounding her eyebrows at the lovelorn crescendo. I'd sit on the bedroom floor across from her, watching her use a sharp pencil to draw her brothers' faces, or sometimes even my father's.

I still think about that notebook sometimes, the only soft memory I have of my mother. It was the only little secret she kept for herself; no other hands ever greased its pages but mine and hers. She brought it with her every time we moved house throughout my childhood. It sat on a shelf in her closet, the pages yellowing, their edges wrinkling, the pictures on them fading slowly. What had happened to it after my parents' divorce? Did my mother take it with her back to her parents' home? Did she keep it with her always? Maybe she retraced the faded linework with a crisp, sharpened pencil to keep the faces alive. Maybe she drew my face from memory.

When she got a day off from her many responsibilities in the home of her in-laws, my mother would visit her own mother's home. She'd wrap a hijab around her head lightly, fussing in front of the mirror to allow a lock of her hair to spill onto her forehead in a way that looked unintentional. My aunts and grandmother disapproved of her long skirts and blouses patterned with stripes and shapes and loud colours, preferring their own long black jackets and tightly wrapped white hijabs for short trips outside the house. Their outfits looked suffocating to me, especially on hot summer afternoons.

Some days my mother took me along on her weekly visit, and on others she left me under the watchful eyes of my grandmother and aunts. On one such occasion, I stood by the kitchen door looking on as the women gathered around the table to remove the caps of okra beans and skin tomatoes for dinner. My grandmother and aunts chit-chatted listlessly and gossiped about neighbours' marriages and pregnancies. Although my youngest aunt was just three or four years older than me, she assumed a womanly role at the kitchen table.

"Come, what are you doing there?" She summoned me over. "Are you bored?"

I nodded.

"Do you want to learn how to uncap okra?"

I nodded again.

She reached for a dull knife for me to use, but my grandmother was quick to gently slap her hand. "No, he is a boy," my grandmother said. "Boys don't cook."

"He could help in the kitchen," my aunt whined. "It'll take us hours to finish all this okra."

"Do you see any of your brothers helping in the kitchen?" The elder aunt gestured with the tip of her knife toward me. "Tomorrow he'll grow up and become a man like his father and uncles."

"If his father was here he'd take him to work with him," my grandmother added. "That's how you raise a good man." She turned to me. "Go play with your football outside."

I turned silently, then changed my mind and stood by the door. "I'm all alone," I said. "There's no one to play with."

"Maybe we will get him a male cousin to play with." My grandmother eyed her daughters.

"Well, his mother isn't bringing him a brother anytime soon," the elder aunt mumbled, eliciting sighs from the others. "Go play with him for a bit," she told the younger one. "Only for a bit, then come back to help us with the okra."

That night, when my mother returned home, I was already fast asleep in her bedroom, tired from the hours spent playing with my aunt and then following her around while she dusted. When she woke me I saw that she was in her outside clothes but that her hair was uncovered. Her green eyeshadow wrinkled as she frowned.

"I don't want you to tell your grandmother anything anymore." My mother held me by the ear and twisted the soft tissue between the knuckle of her index finger and the tip of her thumb. "Never ever speak a word of us to her ever again."

"I didn't say anything," I whispered.

She gazed at me for a moment and then let go, leaving me with a throbbing pain in my ear. I sat in the corner of my makeshift bed on the floor of her room and watched as she knelt before her own bed and pulled a satchel out from under the mattress. She showed me the bag, the size of her palm, blue, tightened with a red ribbon. It smelled funny and looked as though it were full of stones.

"This is the doing of your grandmother," she told me. "She is cursing me every night. She wants me to die so that she can find a new wife for your father and a new mother for you."

She grabbed my ear again and squeezed it tighter. "Do you understand? Do you want me to die?" she hissed. "She is a witch."

Like all good children, I believed my mother. She taught me never to trim my nails at night and to flush the clippings down the toilet so that they couldn't be used in a magic spell. I watched her clean our combs after every shower so as not to leave our hair for a preying hand. I was so fearful that I trained myself never to sleep past five in the morning, just in case someone else was awake, reciting a magical incantation over me while I slumbered.

I still have trouble sleeping past five in the morning.

HOME

In the spring of 1989, a postman arrived at my grandfather's door and knocked politely. He stood outside with his back to the gateway, indicating his respect for the women of the house, and avoided a direct glimpse into the interior. When he heard my five-year-old voice answering the door, he turned on his heel and asked for the man of the house.

"All the men are at work," I said. My grandmother was quick to step behind me, tightening the gapped door and leaning her covered head through.

"My husband and sons are soon to return home," she said.

"No. They return at—" She pinched my shoulder behind the door. My grandfather wouldn't be home before evening prayers. My uncles and father would probably appear hours after dark, having spent the evening with friends drinking heavy tea, playing backgammon, and smoking argileh in one of the old cafés in the Historic District.

The postman asked my grandmother if she was the wife of Ahmad Ramadan. When she said yes, he offered her an envelope with a government stamp on it. Rather than accept it from his hand, she opened the door wider and pushed a palm against my back so that I'd reach out and grab it. I felt the heavy envelope in my hands, its paper rough to the touch. She quickly pulled me back by my collar, shut the door with a loud thud, and fastened the latch.

"Never tell strangers that our home is empty of men while filled with women and children," she snapped. As my face turned red, she softened her voice. "Ah, child," she said, "you need to learn never to trust strange men."

She ruffled my hair, then whisked the government letter out of my hand. She lifted her reading glasses, forever hanging around her chest like a necklace, ripped the envelope open, and glanced at the pages, covered with lazy signatures and poorly inked stamps.

Then, palm over her lips, she gasped.

The home I grew up in was a two-floor traditional house in the heart of the Sarouja neighbourhood in Damascus. It was subdivided into four humble buildings, each with bedrooms on the second floor and living quarters on the ground, together forming a square around a petite garden. Most of the windows opened to the garden, also known as *Ard Diar*, the homeland. A large shared kitchen, complete with a traditional oven, was located in one of the four buildings, where it took up almost half of the living quarters. The house followed this Mediterranean architectural design to allow light and breeze through the windows but also to protect the women from the eyes of strangers. Sometimes I'd lie on the cold ceramic floors of Ard Diar and watch the tiny little square of sky, pretending I could control the wind as it pushed the clouds in and out of our home's borders.

Al-Salamlek, the men-only zone, intended for guests, took up another large slice of the ground floor: it was lavishly decorated and expensively furnished to impress and gloat. I was rarely allowed in this area, which was cleaned on a weekly basis and reserved for special occasions and big family gatherings.

Tucked deep in the back of another building was *Al-Haramlek*, the women-only zone, where the women of the family could congregate and welcome their female neighbours for afternoon tea. It was smaller and doubled as a family room in the evenings, with an old radio and a new TV. Its seats were low to the ground, and its sole window was high enough that one of my uncles had to climb atop the sofas to open it. Through it, I could see the tips of the homes around us.

"Keep the window open, why don't you?" my grandmother would tell one of my uncles. She exclusively wore her white praying shawl, which doubled as her light dress on hotter days. "It's a gateway for the soul."

Built ten, maybe twelve generations earlier, the house had been in my grandfather's family for over three hundred years. It was normal for such a house to be passed down. My grandfather, the eldest of his brothers, had received it from his father, who'd received it from his father, and so on. Yet the whole family tree had a spiritual connection to it. Each member of the extended family had a tiny share in the house, and if we were to sell it, no one would get more than a couple hundred liras. The long history diluted contracts and paperwork and made the house's actual physical ownership too complicated to name. But instead of becoming a source of conflict and competition, the house became a divine centre for everyone who shared blood with my grandfather, a place where joyful weddings and sorrowful funerals were held, even for family members who were multiple times removed. It was at once shared and private, accessible to all in the extended family, who in turn guarded my grandfather's patriarchal right to call it home.

"You will grow up and be the man of this house," my grandfather had said to me once. "You are the next in the line."

The house was old, and it knew it. There were days when water would seep through the ceilings, even when it wasn't raining. Hidden between layers of dust and hay, humidity created its own maps on the walls with cracks and fractures. Some of the windows were too old to open, while others were too thick to close all the way. Remnants of its history were easily found by a curious child. Brass coffee pots with intricate designs sat on high shelves, too dusty to be used. Pretty wooden chairs with thick velvet coating were too weak to withstand the weight of a human. A gigantic padlock made of rusty iron, useless and locked upon a metal rod, rested against a door frame. No one knew what it was for, or who had its key, yet no one wanted to dispose of it.

Big and majestic as it may have looked to my childhood eyes, the house spoke shyly of the humble status of its people. Curtains were holed and patched, but always clean. Dinners were small and meatless, but festive and joyful. When I would kiss my grandfather's hand and raise it to my forehead to show respect, his skin was rough and splintered.

"Bigger pieces of bread and smaller bites, child," my aunt would say at our dinner table.

Even my Syrian national ID card states that I was born to a family rooted in that neighbourhood, signalling not only my belonging to this home, but also the religion, social status, and class I was born into.

The first in a generation of grandchildren, I was destined at birth to carry the name Ahmad, after my paternal grandfather, who inherited the name from his grandfather, and so on. Like the house, my inherited name would be shared among the grandchildren, both publicly owned and privately mine. As a result of this tradition I also carried my mother's name, a way to distinguish me from my cousins. I grew up Ahmad, the son of Amal.

My grandfather spent weeks flipping through his little phone book, calling every government official he could, trying to change the fate of our home. The letter had informed him that the house was to be seized in order to build a new bridge in downtown Damascus.

"No one I know can do shit about the government!" I heard him shout behind closed doors, my grandmother his only audience. "They want the house. Nothing I can do to change that."

Over the next few months, the men of the family scoured the city for an affordable place to house us all. The mission seemed impossible, as the non-negotiable government compensation for the old family home was laughable in its unfairness. The home that had stood for three hundred years was assessed by government officials as barely livable, its value appraised at a much lower figure than the price of its land. The amount would only just cover three months' rent on a home big enough for our family.

The great sale of all our valuables commenced: my grandfather sold his blacksmith workshop to his partner and became an employee in the business he'd started, while my grandmother, mother, and aunts sold their jewellery. Strangers visited our home, looked through our mosaic-adorned wardrobes, examined our inherited Persian carpets, and flipped channels on our television set. They would haggle, then carry off a prized item after handing the cash to my father or one of my uncles.

We were each allowed an item or two to keep. My mother insisted on her boombox and collection of cassettes; my father kept the back-gammon set he'd bought with his first paycheque after returning from military service. My grandfather clung to his prized family tree canvas, even when one of his cousins offered him a pretty price for it.

"Can I keep my birthday bracelet?" my young aunt asked my grandmother. The gold chain, glittering in the light, looked simple and soft in her palm, adorned with a teddy bear charm.

"That's your decision, daughter," my grandmother said, sorting through a pile of laundry. "I'm selling all my jewellery, and so is your older sister."

My aunt's face crumpled.

"Even this child's mother is doing her part," my grandmother continued, gesturing to me. "But you're a child, daughter. If you want to keep your bracelet like a child, you should."

My aunt's eyes teared. "No. I changed my mind," she said. "You can have it."

"You should give it to one of your brothers." My grandmother busied her hands folding a towel, tucking its middle under her chin. "They'll know what to do."

Even in our last days in the house, the women never abandoned their daily duties of tidying the rooms and the garden. Dried leaves were gathered in corners then stuffed into plastic bags. The fountain's water remained clean, fragrant with jasmine and oleander. The sold furniture revealed pockets of dust that were quickly swept up so that the floors could be mopped.

At the end of 1989 our large family moved into an apartment on the outskirts of Damascus, in a newly formed neighbourhood called Al-Mazeh Jabal, near a mountainous military base called Brigade 86.

We left behind the old chairs that no one wanted to buy, the lemon tree that no one would tend to, the traditional oven never to be lit again, and the rusted lock no one bothered to break.

We weren't the only ones who received the order of eviction. Neighbours who'd borrowed cups of sugar or a needle and a thread were scattered across the city in all directions and soon became a distant memory, like the abandoned chairs. My grandmother tried to keep in touch with a few of them, managing to get their new phone numbers through connections in their old praying circles and mosques. But after the move the phone rang less frequently, and so she busied herself rebuilding her life and the lives of her family in our new home.

The government left the homes abandoned for months after our departure. I imagined ours infested with rats, eating away at the wooden chairs, swimming in the murky waters of the fountain, and building nests on the shelves where I used to organize my toys. A whole strip of old houses in Sarouja waited darkly for months, leaning on one another just as their people had done for years. Until one day the government brought their bulldozers and flattened the whole neighbourhood, trees and all, then expanded a road and built a small bridge on its remains.

If you were to visit our new home back then, you'd have to drive thirty minutes from Sarouja in downtown Damascus, heading west on the highway to Beirut. You'd leave behind the historic corners of the seven-thousand-year-old city—its streets busy with vendors, its many souks smelling of cumin and sandalwood—and be welcomed by empty roads, sparse shops, and buildings under construction. Finally you'd reach Al-Mazeh district. Your car would need to be a well-built automatic or a manual with a strong engine, for you'd have to ascend a steep slope for two or three hundred metres and then turn onto an equally steep side road and park by the fourth building to your right. If you were to take a cab, you'd have to lie and claim you were only going to Al-Mazeh, then test the driver's boundaries to see whether he was willing to climb the hill or whether he'd refuse, dropping you at the foot of the road and forcing you to walk up on your own.

The apartment, on the top floor of a three-storey building, had a modest kitchen, a single bathroom, one bedroom, and a guest room. My grandfather bought sofas that turned into beds for his seven sons and daughters to share in the living room, while my parents and I lived in the guest room, separated from the others by only a thin door of glass and wood. My grandmother hung garlic clusters on the wall by the kitchen window and dried spinach and mulukhiyah leaves by the small white fridge.

The only decoration we had was the family tree canvas, too big to fit in the small living room and destined to live for the rest of time on the wall of the long hallway, too dark for anyone to decipher the names.

To lessen the overcrowding, my father and uncles built a bachelor apartment on the rooftop. Not the best of builders, and lacking the funds to hire professionals, they raised three walls, spiderwebbed the ceiling with metal rods, then covered it with clay roofing tiles. That bachelor became our first independent home as a nuclear family, although we'd continue to share the bathroom and kitchen downstairs until my father could afford to build our own on the rooftop two years later.

The only saving grace of our new living arrangement was the view of Damascus from our vantage point high up on the side of one of its mountains. On sunny days you could see all the way across the city to the mountains that surrounded it like jewels on a crown. The roads through the valley intersected then split off in different directions like the routes of children playing tag. Winds carried the clouds and whipped them into a froth. With the call to the sunset prayer the city turned purple, each building giving its own brushstroke of the majestic colour. Come evening, the mosque minarets across the city would be lit up green, a uniting colour, all pointing toward the Umayyad Mosque at the centre of Damascus, the third in a holy trilogy of Islamic mosques. Their lights would stay on until after dawn, dotting the city and projecting a dim glow onto the mud-coloured ceiling of our home.

My father, a ginger-haired man who'd inherited his green eyes from the days of the region's Ottoman occupation, proudly invited friends and extended family to his new home. His voice would boom throughout the little apartment late into the night as he discussed the matters of the day and stated his opinions firmly, keeping politics and religion out of the conversation. He was in his mid-twenties then: a child pretending to be an adult. Still, he charmed our new neighbours with his soft manners and good looks. Soon he'd built a circle of friends that visited on a steady rotation and offered gifts during religious holidays.

On summer nights he'd invite the whole family to join us on the rooftop, bringing grapes, slices of watermelon, grilled sunflower seeds, and heavy pots of tea. He overspent on these nights, sometimes leaving us with no budget to buy our necessities for the next few days. And yet he relished his status as the first of his brothers to marry and provide grandchildren. Even with no house to be inherited, he took pride in knowing that his son would be the carrier of the family name and the leader of the next generation.

I kept to myself on these nights. In my own corner of the world, with nothing between me and the sky, I could imagine we were back in the garden of our old home. My mother would bring out her boombox and my aunt would insert a cassette, playing songs by the Egyptian singer Umm Kulthum until I could barely keep my eyes open.

Over time these gatherings became less frequent. When they did happen, the music's volume would be hushed and the offerings on the dinner table would be less extravagant. Within a year, dinners had been replaced by polite coffees and cheaply made desserts. Instead of new clothes for Eid, we would patch the old ones. Instead of a new uniform for my first year of school, I'd inherit one from a neighbour.

My extended family's slip from its working-class status down to the poverty line wasn't unheard of across Syria at the time. Since 1986 the country had been under economic and political sanctions imposed by the U.S. administration, sanctions that had slowly caused an economic ripple effect that trickled down. Lines outside of government-owned bakeries swelled, and goods such as sugar, eggs, wheat, and rice fell under government control. Each household was rationed items based on the number of family members and their ages. Once a month I would accompany one of the men of the house to the government-run store and stand in line for hours. Officials would stamp our IDs with the date and issue our flat of eggs along with lumpy bags of sugar and brown rice dotted with dead ants. When cigarettes became extremely expensive, my uncles either quit smoking or switched to the locally made Al-Hamra brand, infamous for its poorly mixed tobacco and chemical smell.

A bit over a year in that new home, my grandfather complained of a mysterious pain in his chest and limbs but couldn't afford taking a break from work for a doctor's visit. Weeks later we woke up to an ambulance siren, and I never saw my grandfather again.

I wonder if my grandfather died of a broken heart. Maybe he couldn't bear to live so far away from the place he'd called home since the day he was born and felt estranged from the place where he'd been forced to relocate. Was he a caged tiger, unable to handle the diminished life he'd been cornered into? In his old house he welcomed members of our extended family every other night, hosting their weddings and ordering around his women to clean and to prepare traditional desserts. But in the new apartment he barely had room for himself and his wife, what with the rest of the house crowded with sofa beds and mattresses for his many children. I wonder if he felt like a refugee in his own home.

I have very few memories of my grandfather. He spent most of his days at work, and he died before I was old enough to remember him in his day-to-day life. Instead, I have glimpses: I see him standing in his traditional white outfit, singing Islamic rhymes on the prophet's birthday, surrounded by his children. I recall sitting on his lap while he told me of the prophet's spiritual journey to heaven and hell on the day of the holy Isra' and Mi'raj, naming the many blisses offered by Allah to those who obey him, and the punishments that await those who defy. I remember him untying a small bag of sugar-covered almonds and handing me three: one white, one blue, and one pink.

Maybe he died of the shame that he couldn't pass the house to his eldest grandson, as the many grandfathers in his bloodline had done before him. Maybe he couldn't bear to be the last of his name to live in that home, to be the one associated with its destruction.

My grandfather's passing brought on a conflict among his children. My uncles, many of them ready to take the step to which my father had outraced them, wanted a similar piece of the apartment where they could bring their own wives and raise their own children. This wouldn't have been a problem at the old place, with its many rooms for housing the next generations. But in the new house it was a nearly impossible task.

Soon, both of my aunts were hastily married and left our home. My father and uncles built a wall in the middle of our rooftop apartment, dividing it into two and creating a place for one of my older uncles and his new wife.

Our small rooftop home did, though, bring some joy into my parents' marriage. My mother decorated the open-concept space as she pleased. She decided on wallpaper—yellow, with a pattern of flower bouquets—hung dream catchers from the metal rods in the ceiling, and situated the TV so that they could watch it from the sofa or their bed. I grew too big for my own bed, but it was our only option: I slept there cradling my knees, cocooned like a child in a womb.

My mother lulled her demons and found a balance in her mind. Did they find her the right therapist? Was it the independence she finally received? Two years passed in a semi-calm, and she got pregnant and gave birth to Nour in 1991. Then, almost instantly, she got pregnant again. Now my father tiptoed around her, bringing her all the fruits she craved. He even showed up for lunches and dinners and discussed the family affairs openly.

One afternoon we were sitting around the table—my father at the head, my mother feeding Nour in her lap, and me eating silently at the opposite end—when I heard water splashing. At first I thought Nour must have knocked a glass over, but then I realized that my mother's pyjamas were soaking wet.

"Did Nour pee herself?" I asked.

My mother lifted the baby off her lap, stared at her own lower half, then snapped into action. She handed Nour to my dazed father and rushed to the bathroom. My father handed me the baby in turn and ran after her.

"Did your water break?" I heard him asking.

"It's not time yet!" she wailed from inside the bathroom.

I was left with my grandmother downstairs while an uncle drove my parents to the hospital. They spent the night away and I slept on the floor in my grandmother's bedroom.

The next morning my father called. He talked to his mother and she whispered back to him. I heard her repeat the name of Allah. Allah this and Allah that. Allah's will, Allah's fate, Allah's heaven, Allah's decision. Then my grandmother handed me the phone.

"Hey, you okay?" my father asked.

"What happened to Mama?"

"She lost the baby."

"Why?"

"I don't know."

"Was it a boy or a girl?"

"It was a girl."

"Oh." I paused. "Is she dead?"

"Who?"

"The baby."

"Yeah. She is dead."

"Why?"

"I don't know."

"How big was she?"

"As big as a peach. Why do you ask?"

"She couldn't be bigger? If she was bigger, she might have lived."

"No. She couldn't be bigger."

"Can I see her?"

"The baby?"

"No. Mama."

"Soon."

A couple of days later a silent, bushy-haired, dazed version of my mother came back from the hospital. Within weeks, her old ways returned. She threw glass bottles of milk across the kitchen at ghosts and ghouls she claimed came to seduce her. One of the bottles smashed into my left hand, resulting in a visit to the hospital, multiple stitches, and a permanent scar between my middle and ring fingers. My father got home from work to find his two birds of paradise dead on the floor of their birdcage, their lives snuffed out and their necks snapped, punished for being carriers of a mysterious virus that my mother believed had caused the miscarriage.

The final straw came when we woke in the middle of the night to screaming.

I could also hear the baby crying in her crib, my only light the dying fire in the small radiant gas heater. My father had already jumped out of bed and run through the open gate. I followed him barefoot as he descended the stairs to my grandmother's house.

"You've cursed me!" we heard my mother shouting. "You've killed my baby!"

I watched from the top of the stairs as my father grabbed her by the elbow and tried to pull her back home. The door opened and my grandmother and two uncles appeared, eyes heavy with sleep.

"What's going on now?" my grandmother shouted back.

My uncle came down the stairs with his new wife and stood behind me, placing a hand on my shoulder to direct me back to bed, but I brushed his hand off.

"Your mother is a witch!" my mother continued. "She killed our child!"

"Come back to bed now," my father said firmly. An uncle stood between my mother and his. "Come back or else I will divorce you on the spot."

My mother pulled at her nightgown, stretching and then tearing the fabric. She howled like an animal and stepped toward my grandmother, hands extended, but my father pulled her back.

"I told you not to marry her," my grandmother said. "She's as crazy as her mother."

My uncle stepped down the stairs and then both men dragged my mother back up to our apartment, screaming and shouting and ripping her own clothes. My father locked the door and stood guard while my mother lay on the bed, crying.

Days later, the men in the family came together and agreed that separating my mother from her in-laws would be for the best. They decided it was time for my father to sell his share of the apartment to one of his brothers, and for us to move to a home of our own.

BOYHOOD

I stood on the rooftop of our old home and called out the name of my friend.

Our neighbour's daughter, Nevene, had borrowed something of mine, and we were packing to leave this home forever. Was it the children's book my aunt got me for my birthday? The blue stuffed horse my grandfather brought back from Saudi Arabia after his Hajj the year before? That box of colourful crayons? Who can say.

The hymns of nearby traffic swept the otherwise silent neighbourhood. I stood by the short perimeter wall dividing our property from theirs, high enough to be at my eye level.

"Neeveene!" I stressed the high-pitched sounds in her name and then called it again, forming a horn with my palms. "Neeeeeeeeeee-veeeeeeeeeene!"

I hooked my hands onto the top of the wall and stood on my toes to see the other side. I held my breath, listening for footsteps. Instead the footsteps came from behind. Startled, I jumped back to avoid my father's hand. He called those unannounced slaps to my neck "airplanes."

"What the hell are you doing?" My father crouched to meet me at my height. "What kind of noise were you making?"

"I was calling her name."

"You yell like a girl." He put his hands on my shoulders and squeezed. "Never shout like this again, you hear me? Men shout like this, son." He stood up, rounded his chest, rolled his shoulders back, lifted his chin high, and barked like an angry dog.

"NEVENE!"

He looked down at me and asked me to try.

"Neeveene?"

"No, you idiot. Don't wail like a woman. Command it, like the man you are. NEVENE!"

I made another attempt.

"Louder."

"Nevene!"

"I said louder!"

"NEVENE!"

"What?" Nevene's voice came from the other end of the rooftop. My father looked away while Nevene's mother, who'd joined her to investigate all the yelling, tightened the hijab over her head.

Was this my father's first glimpse of my queerness? The moment he began trying to surgically remove my feminine qualities? I'm sure that in his mind he was doing me a favour. It's unlikely that he thought of it in these terms, but it's possible he detected my queerness long before I did and worried about what kind of future I'd have in an Islamic society with homophobic laws. Maybe this was his way of showing love? Love comes in all shapes and sizes—maybe this was his unique way of ensuring I wouldn't suffer as a result of being different from everyone else.

Or maybe he feared that my homosexuality would reflect poorly on my family, on his own masculinity, and on his ability to raise a child properly—what would the community think if he raised a soft, effeminate child? But if keeping up appearances was the reason, I wonder why he focused on my homosexuality and not on the other dysfunctional aspects of our little family unit.

Or maybe—and this is a big maybe—none of it matters. This tension is in my head and no one else's. It was the response of a typical Syrian father to an atypical Syrian child, and no matter what he did I wouldn't have found love in that relationship.

Over the next few years my father would try to toughen me up with many other activities. He placed me in an Islamic after-school group and insisted I try my hand at boxing. At age twelve I attended classes for a six-month stint, returning home with a black eye every other night.

"I throw a mean left hook," I joke to this day, "but I still love dick."

Syria, it must be said, is a homophobic country.

Now that we've gotten that out of our system, let's try to complicate this narrative a bit. For most of its history, homosexual acts were normalized and celebrated in the geographical region now known as Syria. Even during the Islamic era, Abu Nuwas, who in the eighth century lived in what is now Iraq, wrote explicitly about his homosexuality and many male lovers. *I die of love for him, perfect in every way*, one of his poems reads. *Lost in the strains of wafting music. /*

My eyes are fixed upon his delightful body / And I do not wonder at his beauty. / His waist is a sapling, his face a moon, / And loveliness rolls off his rosy cheek. / I die of love for you, but keep this secret: / The tie that binds us is an unbreakable rope.

Throughout the thirteenth and fourteenth centuries, poets like Rumi and Hafiz, who lived in what is now Iran, mused about their same-sex desires in verse. *If anyone asks you / how the perfect satisfaction / of all our sexual wanting / will look*, Rumi wrote, using the male indications in gendering both pronouns and verbs found in Old Persian, *lift your face / and say, / Like this.*

Under the Ottoman Empire, ruling all the way from Istanbul, homosexuality was legalized in Syria up until the late eighteenth century, and gay male partnerships were recognized in legal matters such as inheritance and bloodlines. Even in the late twentieth century Syrian playwright Saadallah Wannous could publish his *Rituals of Signs and Transformations*, a play depicting homosexuality in a semipositive light: as a torment of the mind rather than a sin of the body.

Of course, Syria views the subject of homosexuality quite differently now. Abu Nuwas's poetry is banned, and the work of Rumi and Hafiz is highly edited and redacted; we rarely learn anything about the history of the Ottoman occupation, let alone its homosexual tendencies, and you'd be hard-pressed to find a copy of Wannous's homoerotic works. Homosexual acts are de facto punished by three years in prison and public shaming in our courts of law.

So what happened? Well, colonization.

In 1885 the British government introduced the Criminal Law Amendment Act, which included much stricter penal codes that punished all homosexual behaviours. It was an update to the Buggery

Act, passed in 1533 under King Henry VIII. The British Parliament and the Church were at odds at the time, and homosexual acts became a scapegoat for the former in a bid to show virtue to the people and win back confidence from the Church. The French government was quick to mirror the act, borrowing much of its wording, including its laws even against homosexual tendencies. A loving letter between two male friends, for example, was enough of an indication of homosexuality and became punishable by law. I assume many Frenchmen found that distasteful.

Of the nearly eighty countries that criminalize homosexuality today, two-thirds are former British and French colonies. After the Allies defeated the Ottoman Empire in World War I they divided the riches and gave modern-day Syria to the French, who came in with their constitutions and homophobic laws. Even after their departure following World War II, the French constitution became the basis of the Syrian one, and the penal codes punishing homosexuality remain in our laws to this day.

To make matters worse was the rise of Islamic fundamentalism in the seventies and eighties, coinciding with the gay rights movement in North America and Europe. And yet, oddly, Islamists left the gays alone: they focused on critically and logistically targeting the political dictatorship rather than the social fabric of the community to which they were endearing themselves. Smart Arab dictators, on the other hand, tried to appease their people by stoking anti-gay societal values through scandalous stories and fear-based propaganda. Once again, the politicians used queer and trans people as scapegoats to project a modern Islam front with a traditional bent, countering the hardline fundamentalist groups while at the same time standing up for Arabism against the infidel West and its drag queens. Homophobia became a nationalistic moral, and queers became a target in their societies of birth.

●

"If the number is even, God will help me," I said to myself on my way back from school. "If it's odd, I am doomed to hell."

I was retracing my steps, counting them one after the other as I returned to our new home. My outfit was beige and my neckerchief was blue with a white stripe, indicating that I was in fifth grade. I tightened my stride, keeping a close count in my head.

"Seven hundred and twenty-two, twenty-three, twenty-four, twenty-five."

The only term I'd heard to describe my sexual predicament was *Louti*—meaning the people of Lut, the Islamic prophet sent to Sodom and Gomorrah to preach to their inhabitants about the sinfulness of homosexuality. On Fridays at the mosque, I'd sit cross-legged on the carpet, looking up at the imam in his little minbar, the pulpit where he stood to deliver sermons. He told the stories of prophets like Lut, narratives that followed a typical formula: a middle-aged man of humble beginnings is offered guidance from Allah through one of his angels. The prophet is sent to such-and-such community, but his people pay no heed to his warnings and instead threaten him with punishment. After a final test of some sort, Allah instructs the prophet to take what followers he has and leave the community, whose members are subsequently destroyed in a miraculous retribution. The sentence of choice for Sodom and Gomorrah is narrated in the Quran: "We turned [the cities] upside down, and rained down on them brimstones hard as baked clay, spread, layer on layer."

If you've heard the story of one prophet, you've heard them all.

"Ninety-seven," I counted, climbing up the unpaved road to our home in the mountain slums. "Ninety-eight, ninety-nine, eight hundred."

I had bought a book of Islamic prayers and recited one a hundred times the night before. "Oh Allah, I seek refuge in You from affliction, misery, and bad judgment," I sang. "I pray Your grace won't be demised and Your blessing won't dissipate. I fear the suddenness of Your vengeance, and all of Your anger."

I'd closed my eyes, wondering if Allah would hear my prayer, and when I awoke in the morning I'd decided on this method of finding out. "One thousand one hundred and one, one hundred and two, one hundred and three."

Our new home was not yet suitable for occupation. Windowpanes were missing, replaced by taped plastic bags. The rough concrete and brick walls remained unpainted. But I'd been offered my own room for the first time and spent most days hiding there, reading and rereading Egyptian YA novels that glamorized the North African country and trumpeted nationalistic narratives.

"Two thousand five hundred and seventy-seven. Seventy-eight, seventy-nine." I was almost at the building's gate; two more steps would get me there. I paused, then stretched my leg as far as it would go, reaching the gate's frame with my toes. "Eighty!" I smiled. Clearly, I wouldn't go to hell.

The next day at school, though, I was still in love with Ayman.

Although I didn't name it at the time, I'd been in love with Ayman since second grade. He was a quiet child with soulful eyes who enjoyed drawing. I don't recall him using crayons or markers, only a sharpened pencil, held at an angle to render whatever image he was conjuring with depth and shadow. His hands moved with grace, as opposed to others around him, who held their markers in a fist and drew endless circles, denting the pages.

I hardly remember a thing about any of my schoolmates. Ayman, on the other hand, I remember clearly. His black hair, the reading glasses he'd worn ever since I met him. His crooked teeth, which he fixed over the years with expensive braces. His long neck, which I admired from my seat at the back of the classroom. Smooth in earlier years, then eventually lined with hair, like two black waterfalls spilling down. He always outran me to maturity; the hair on his arms and upper lip grew months before mine, and he shot up in fifth grade while I remained at my child's height until eighth.

Ayman and I were never really friends. He knew me, but he always hung out with his two best friends. The three of them, all from upper-class families, with shiny uniforms and branded school bags, came and went together.

"The only way for you to join our group is to pass a series of tests," one of his friends told me when I gathered the strength to introduce myself in the schoolyard. "We'll each have a test for you."

I nodded in agreement. I can picture my eleven-year-old self: eager to please, starving for love, breathlessly devoted to a friend who barely knew I existed.

The first was a test of trickery. "You have to go to the cafeteria and buy a bottle of soda with this fake money." Ayman's friend handed me a piece of paper torn out of a notebook, a clumsy counterfeiting attempt drawn on it. "Come back with the soda and you shall join us."

I took the paper and eyed the three of them. Ayman matched his friends' wicked smiles. I turned and ran to the cafeteria, switching the fake paper with real money on the way—the only five pounds I had for the day, barely enough to buy the drink. Minutes later, I returned victorious.

"Did you pay with the fake money?" one of the friends asked.

"Of course."

"That's a lie. I followed you. You paid with real money." He grabbed the drink out of my hand and downed it. "You failed your test. You will never be part of our group."

"No, I paid with the paper you gave me," I pressed. The boy laughed and ushered his friends away.

"Wait—" Ayman said. "*Did* he fail the test, though? It was a test of trickery, and he did attempt to trick us."

"Don't be an idiot," the friend said. "Come on, let's go."

Ayman gave me a sympathetic look and followed his friends.

When Ayman was alone, he sometimes talked to me. (And over the years he would borrow books from the library I'd amassed using my weekly allowance, filling my shelves first with children's books, then with simplified translations of British, French, and Russian literature.) He would share his homemade cakes with me, too, as long as his two best friends weren't looking.

"Ahmad! Wait!" I heard him calling my name as I walked home alone. I stood, my heart racing, and waited for him. "I wanted to ask you something."

He caught up to me and squeezed under my umbrella. I raised my hand so that his head fit under it, and we walked shoulder to shoulder. "How come you're so good at English?" he asked.

"Oh." I paused, embarrassed. I'd discovered American and British boy bands a year or two earlier, and since then had obsessively researched their lyrics and sang their songs in my head. "I don't know. Why?"

"I was wondering if you'd help me with my English homework," he said. "I can come over to your place one afternoon and we can work on it together."

"I can come over to yours." I couldn't imagine Ayman walking into our embarrassingly poor neighbourhood and hanging out in my unpainted bedroom.

"I share my bedroom with my brother. It's better at yours," he insisted. I nodded, and he promised to come over that evening.

I waited until he disappeared in the direction of his home, then ran. I made it home breathless and spent the rest of the afternoon cleaning. My mother dozed off in her bedroom and my sisters promised to keep it down. Eyes on the clock, I plumped pillows and wiped down tabletops, then used the vacuum cleaner on the dust and got tangled in its cord. Then, an hour before Ayman's promised arrival time, I took a cold shower and lathered my body with my mother's soap. By the time the clock struck six I was sitting patiently by the window, waiting. The clock's hands swirled around; seconds turned to minutes. Maybe he got lost? Maybe he saw the neighbourhood and decided to turn around, never to return. Maybe he no longer needed help with his homework. I waited at the window for what felt like hours, but Ayman never showed. The next day I caught him alone in the schoolyard and asked what had happened.

"Oh, I forgot." He quickly waved me away and joined his two best friends. After that I didn't see much of Ayman. As we grew older he borrowed books less often, until he stopped altogether. Our secondary educations took us in different directions, him to a private institute and me to a public school.

∙

In my early teen years, I regularly escaped home to one of the many mosques in the neighbourhood.

The Islamic narrative around who I was growing up to be did not endear me much to the religion. I was torn between the peacefulness a mosque offered and the harsh words its imam spoke. I loved the softness of the carpet on my feet, the quietude of so many bodies together in silence and moving in unison. The empty minbar made me feel purer, as if I could look up and create a direct link between Allah and me, carry on a private conversation in whispers. I started to visit mosques in the off hours, when no prayer was called. I'd wash my face, arms, and feet in their fountains and then walk with my wet socks on their hot ceramic backyards and spend afternoons resting my head against their columns, murmuring the words of the Quran like poetry, sometimes even taking an unintended nap.

Then, as if through divine intervention, I stumbled upon some much-needed guidance.

In the early nineties, on Friday afternoons, overlapping with the noon prayers that gather all devoted Muslims for the weekly ceremony, a variety show played on one of our two TV channels. The program was dumped into the ninety minutes of dead airtime when men and women were out of their homes and at prayer. Its title was a tongue-in-cheek reference to a Rumi poem, and it was hosted by an older gentleman who read poetry, screened clips from Western movies and TV shows, described Broadway musicals, and marvelled over opera performances.

I used to walk with my father to the Friday prayers, elude him at the busy mosque gate, and rush back home to catch the show. I would watch as the presenter played pirated clips from a Yanni concert at the Acropolis or a recording of "Sit Down, You're Rockin' the Boat" from *Guys and Dolls* and swoon over the music and its orchestration.

The show ran for only two years before the host abandoned it and left the country. I never learned more about him, but the queerness of his work shaped me in immeasurable ways; I was mesmerized by the art he brought to my screen and tickled by the thrill of watching it when no one else was around.

One day, the presenter was coy as he cued up the next movie clip. "This comedy swept the West a couple of years ago and won many awards," he said. "It tells a story of a man who has to fit into his rigid little town." He didn't offer the movie's title. In the scene, a handsome man attempts to rein in his effeminate mannerisms and appear more masculine, but he fails miserably when a disco track plays on the radio, compelling him into a swishy dance.

I didn't recognize it at the time, but the scene was from the 1997 film *In & Out* starring Kevin Kline. Kline plays a small-town English teacher whose former student unwittingly outs him in an Oscar acceptance speech before he's even out to himself. The character spends most of the movie trying to correct the misunderstanding before coming to realize, accept, and even celebrate his homosexuality.

I was twelve—maybe thirteen—when I watched that pivotal clip on that local TV station in Damascus, hiding in our living room while the call for prayer echoed across the city. I didn't come to any explicit realizations about my own sexuality in that moment, but watching this man question his own masculinity, then celebrate his unique gender expression through flamboyant dance, felt comforting. It felt like an answer to a question I didn't know how to ask.

I wouldn't encounter an actual living, breathing gay person till I was fifteen.

My extended family had gathered their resources and rented a two-bedroom waterfront cottage on the sands of the Mediterranean. Eighteen of us—uncles, aunts, brothers, sisters, in-laws, cousins, grandparents—boarded a bus and drove six hours from Damascus to Latakia, famous for its clear waters and white-sand beaches. The cottage was too small for us. Our luggage took up much of the living room, and snappy comments flew on who would sleep where. Its doors slid open to a small ground-floor terrace with sand lining its tiles and hammocks hanging by its walls. Children ran to dip their toes in the water while the adults argued.

Days were spent at the beach; nights were filled with the crackling of overused cassette tapes playing the same Fairuz and Umm

Kulthum songs. I turned golden in the sun and dripped a trail of sand wherever I went. Lulled by the waves, I slept in a hammock on the terrace, happily separated from my bickering parents.

On a cloudy afternoon, my uncles and I played basketball in the cement court by the cottage. To expel my never-ending energy my uncles tasked me with attempting to score a three-pointer, knowing well that I was too short to do so. I spent the afternoon making attempts on one side of the court while the four of them played on the other.

That's when I saw them.

There were five in total. To me they looked like full-fledged adults, but they couldn't have been much older than twenty-five. They wore tight swimming shorts and had wrapped their torsos with silky shawls I'd only ever seen on women. They pushed one another playfully, giggled loudly, and called one another's names with the sharpness I'd been punished for as a child. My uncles paused their game, flashing dirty looks that quickly drove them away.

"I think I'll go for a walk," I told my uncles.

"Where?" one of them asked.

I gestured vaguely toward the sunset. My eldest uncle, a tall man who wore a toupée, stopped playing, held the basketball in his hand, and looked me straight in the eyes.

"You want to follow those boys, don't you?"

"No."

"Then where are you going?"

"There." I pointed in the opposite direction.

"Why?"

"Because I want to."

He paused, looked at his brothers, then back at me. "Okay," he said, "you can go for a walk. But don't be long."

I rushed in the opposite direction from where the boys had gone. Then, at what I hoped was a far enough distance from the basketball court, I took a sharp turn and began following their path. I peeked from behind the wall of a chalet and saw that my uncles had resumed their game.

But when I made it to the beach, safe from the eyes of relatives, I couldn't find the boys. I looked around until the first stars dotted the sky. Disappointed, I returned to the basketball court to find it empty. Back at the cottage everyone was gathered on the terrace, cracking sunflower seeds and eating watermelon.

"You were gone for too long." My uncle held his eyes on me, as if searching for evidence of foul play.

"No, I wasn't," I said and ran inside. He never brought it up again.

I dreamt that night that I found them. I dreamt that we spent the afternoon talking. That one of them held my hand. During our final two days in Latakia I kept my eye on the seashore, but they never reappeared.

When I returned to Damascus, I told Joseph about all of this.

I wouldn't call Joseph a friend—our relationship was transactional. He was a distant neighbour who once saw me walking home with a selection of the Egyptian YA novels in my arms and approached me. He owned some of the books I was missing in the series and borrowed some of mine.

Joseph was all I had. He was three years older than me, with dimples and curly black hair. He laughed at things I didn't find funny, chewed his food loud enough to wake the dead, and owned a single pair of shoes that constantly accrued new holes and dirt. When I borrowed his books, I noticed that he'd used a coin to scratch the characters' faces off the covers, which he explained was for religious reasons. I was too polite to ask for further explanation.

Joseph lived with his single mother in a two-bedroom apartment up the slums hill. She was never home, regardless of the hour of the day I visited. They had a big-screen TV and a VCR in their living room, where we watched video rentals—*The Mummy*, *Batman & Robin*. Other times we played Madonna or Michael Jackson on the stereo or tuned in to the Lebanese channels, catching episodes of *Star Trek: Voyager* and *Xena: Warrior Princess*.

Joseph always sat close while we watched movies, his thigh brushing against mine. He'd draw the curtains and turn off the lights, insisting on the cinematic effect of darkness.

"Why were you so interested in these boys?"

"I don't know," I said. "I wanted to know them."

"Yeah, but why?"

"I don't know."

"Have you ever watched porn?" he asked me point-blank.

Boys at school had snuck in magazine clippings they'd found in their parents' dresser drawers or under their mattresses: photos of women in various exposed positions, smiling invitingly or innocently, depending on the direction of the photo shoot. I echoed the other boys' excitement, mirrored the wonder in their eyes, but it was an act.

I told him I hadn't.

Joseph asked me to stand up, then lifted the cushion I'd been sitting on and dug his arm into the couch. After a moment of fumbling, he fished out a black VHS tape with no label.

"Sit down. Watch this."

He inserted the tape, and soon a cheesy, amateur beat filled the room. We sat next to each other in silence, watching.

A large-bosomed woman answered the door and instructed a delivery man to put the pizza boxes on a kitchen counter. After an exchange of overacted dialogue, she was on her knees sucking him off. The man, who based on looks alone could never dream of scoring an encounter with such a beautiful woman, sat back on a bar stool and lifted her skirt to reveal the sexy lingerie underneath her housewife attire.

"Where did you get this?" I asked.

"What do you think?"

The man on TV moaned in ecstasy.

My jaw tensed; I had trouble swallowing. I leaned back and exhaled. "How could he be enjoying that?"

Then I felt Joseph's breath on my neck before he gently bit my earlobe. I froze as he began to use his tongue. He kept his hands to himself, and so did I. I turned to face him, our lips inches apart, and leaned forward for a kiss, but he dodged it. I followed his lips, but he gently held me back. "No," he whispered. He pushed me down on the sofa and got on top of me, kissing the root of my neck, cupping my chest, and resting his hips between my legs. I felt his body, hot to the touch, over his clothes, then lifted his shirt and inserted my hands underneath to caress his torso. I tried to kiss his lips again, but he squeezed them shut and directed my face toward his shoulders. I kissed him there for a while, feeling myself grow against my jeans.

We continued in this way, never going under the belt, never removing our shirts. His weight on my body felt nice, and in his arms I felt secure. The tension in my jaw released.

When the tape ended, a static noise filled the room. Annoyed, Joseph got up from the sofa and turned off the VCR. I lifted myself up and adjusted my T-shirt. The two of us were silent for a while.

"I like women," he said finally. "I like to touch their boobs and squeeze as if I'm tuning an old radio's dial." He locked eyes with me. "Do you understand?"

I nodded, quickly excused myself, and left.

Over the next six months our experimenting progressed: We kissed each other's shirtless bodies; I bit his nipples; we felt each other up on the couch while watching a movie; we stroked each other over our underwear in his bed. Finally, on a cold winter night months later, we got fully naked together. But we never kissed once, as per his wishes. Perhaps in his mind, by keeping his lips virgin he was maintaining his heterosexuality. After that winter night our encounters grew further apart, until eventually they fizzled out entirely.

I still think about Joseph from time to time. I wonder where in the world he ended up after I lost touch with him a good twenty years ago. Sometimes, when I'm invited to high school lectures and LGBTQ+ student symposiums, I bring a version of him up on stage with me. In Canada I'm sought out by teachers hungry for stories of individuals finding their true selves despite the obstacles. And so during these visits I tell this story differently. I spin a tale of a loving first boyfriend who showed me tenderness and protected me from bullies. I justify this lie to myself. Who wants to hear a story of scarcity? What message would I be sharing with these young folks if I told them that my first encounter was actually devoid of the intimacy I craved? Instead I tell them of a romance fit for a Disney film, as though we all have the luxury of choice, of waiting around for the right person. And within this fabricated story is nested my true message to the students: You deserve love. If a gay man on the other side of the world found love in a homophobic country and in a homophobic time, you can, too.

Teachers applaud. Students ask me to sign their books. Queer youngsters whisper to me in counsellors' offices that they feel better about the world. My job is done.

In truth, I never liked Joseph. I did, however, learn something from him. When we met I was a child longing for tenderness, never having received it from his mentally ill mother or absent father. Our encounters taught me that I could fabricate intimacy through being desired, that I could feel valued for my body. In my child's mind, I had started to believe I wasn't worthy of love. But as a sexual being, I was hugged, touched, embraced. Tongue in my ear, kisses on my shoulder. A new and misguided concept of what it meant to be loved rooted in my mind. This idea grew like a crooked tooth, attempting to accomplish a noble task but instead pressing against the others, misshaping the mouth.

NAMESAKE

The sun is out in Vancouver: a rare sight on a winter's day.

Matthew asks if I'm up for a walk; I remove my headphones, turn off my PlayStation, and nod. We leash the dog, bundle up, and out to the seawall we go. The dog lunges at the gathering geese and they hiss in annoyance. The grass is wet, and his little paws get soaked.

I burrow into Matthew's side. He's a few inches taller than me, a fact I'd half joke that I was bothered by. The colour of his eyes morphs with the weather: hazel on cloudy days, green on rainy ones. Today they pick up a calm blue of the ocean.

At Starbucks, I order my usual. *Caramel macchiato, as it comes.* Short and sweet. Matthew converses with the barista, explaining that he used to be a partner (a fancy way of saying he worked at Starbucks in his youth). He orders his double-shot on ice with soy milk instead of two percent.

"Iced coffee in winter?"

"I'm gay, okay?" he jokes. "I need this to survive."

The barista locks eyes with me and mumbles something.

"Huh?"

"The name on the order?"

"Ah! Danny!"

In typical fashion, the scribbled name that ultimately graces my cup is mangled, nearly unreadable.

"Adani? Do you think this says Adani?" I raise the cup to Matthew's eye level. He examines it, then laughs.

"It sure does."

"So, a brown man like me can't have a Western name like Danny?"

"Don't be sensitive. This is Starbucks. Rumour has it they fuck up names intentionally for the free social media advertisements. It's practically company policy," Matthew says. "Maybe next time just say Ahmad and see where that goes."

I tense. I forget sometimes that I was born Ahmad. That person feels like a variant of me in some other time-space continuum. Maybe a Syrian man who never shouted in his father's face and blurted out that he's gay. A man who accepted his fate the same way most queer men across the Middle East do.

"Maybe this Ahmad character grew up the way a Syrian man is expected to," I say. "Found a job and a wife and raised an endless number of children."

"Where's this coming from?"

"I wonder if he tried to pray the gay away to Allah five times a day. If he cheated on his wife with random strangers in parking lots and alleyways."

"You're being weird."

"You know what's weird?" I ask, the start of an inside joke he knows well.

"What?" he asks, playing into it.

"How much I love your butt."

We laugh, but the image of this alternate-reality Ahmad remains for days after. Is this Ahmad a happier man? Is he closer to his father? Comfortable in his skin and with his choices? Does he, in turn, wonder about me? Does he imagine an alternate version of himself living a Western queer life with a new name, a tall husband, and a loving dog?

I down my coffee before it gets cold.

●

At sixteen, I was still Ahmad, and I hadn't yet thought much about what future versions of myself were possible.

I ran away a lot. Not that anyone would have noticed my disappearance. I spent whatever money I could get at internet cafés. In Syria, many news sites, search engines, and foreign websites were blocked. We had access to a couple of government-run news agencies, most of the Arab online forums, and porn. Rumours circulated that every click you made was monitored by the government, driven by the now entrenched reports of phone calls being recorded and mail being opened. I took what I could get. A quick search had led me to an Egyptian internet forum dedicated to discussions of the YA novels I loved, but mostly I spent evenings talking to strangers in Yahoo chat rooms.

Impressed by my fast typing, the owner of the café offered me a part-time job that would grow into a full-time one when I finished high school. I'd receive the handwritten theses of students from nearby universities, and I'd type them up into Word documents in both Arabic and English. It was a sweet deal: I made pocket money and had free access to the internet all day long. I spent hours on the work, and then on my break I'd slip into a chat room and circle the possibility of meeting other queer men in Damascus.

That's how I met Adnan.

He was in his late forties. He struck up a conversation with me and we exchanged email addresses. He wrote me every day; I'd volley back lengthy replies. When he mentioned his love of poetry, I shared my writing: snippets of verse half stolen from poets I adored, short stories fueled by my childhood trauma and my confusion about where life was taking me, and pages-long fan-fiction novellas narrating the adventures of side characters from the YA series I loved. He sent me his photo: a scanned copy of a studio portrait. He was handsome, with brown eyes, long curly hair, and sideburns that slid past his earlobes. I wouldn't learn till later that the photo was from ten years prior.

I dreaded going home, so after a shift at the café I often went deeper into my city. I walked the historic Al-Hamidiyah and Medhat Pasha souqs in the Al-Hariqa neighbourhood, dodging the calls of shopkeepers hawking mosaics and shawls with Bedouin prints. I sat on the mushroom-shaped stones in Bab Tuma park and smoked cigarettes, gazing at the rich folks getting out of their expensive cars and lining up outside the many bars and clubs. I ate shawarma sandwiches while roaming the Yusuf al-Azma Square, looking at movie posters at the cinemas. I once got on a bus to the Fifth Bridge and ended up at Happy Land, the only amusement park in Damascus, where I went on as many rides as I could afford and waved hello to strangers on the carousel.

I was so lonely.

Months after we got to know each other online, Adnan invited me to his home. He lived in Al-Maleki, a well-to-do neighbourhood in the upscale side of Damascus. Gardens circled the many tall buildings like rings and the streets were wider, with palm trees on their corners and fountains of glittering, pristine water in their squares. Traffic lights were respected by drivers and monitored by clean-suited police officers. On a summer evening I stood below Adnan's building and gazed up at its clean walls and vast balconies. I saw myself reflected in the glass door. I looked poor and miserable, my clothes rumpled and my hair a mess.

"Come on up!" Adnan said over the intercom.

When I arrived at the eighteenth floor he was waiting outside the elevator. Then he led me down the hall, almost tiptoeing, before quickly ushering me into his apartment.

"Welcome!" He gave me a bear hug.

I was shaking inside. I didn't know why I was there anymore. Adnan was older than he appeared in his photo—his hair shorter, his sideburns painted with the white of age—but the collared polo shirt he wore, tight around his chest, confirmed that he was in good shape. His apartment was well-lit, outfitted with multiple crystal chandeliers. A comfortable couch faced the largest TV screen I'd ever seen, and adjacent to the living room was an open-concept kitchen with bar stools encircling its island. A set of large glass doors revealed a balcony with a picturesque view of downtown Damascus.

Adnan put an arm around my waist and guided me to the sofa, where we sat silently. My socked toes traced the intricate details on the lush carpet. I felt his eyes examining me.

"Wine or beer?"

"Beer," I said. I'd never had a drop of either, but I wanted to feel older, more self-assured.

He rattled off three types of beer, and I picked one randomly.

"Are you sure?" he asked. "Dark beer is bitter."

"Yes. I love that."

He fetched a bottle from the fridge and poured himself a glass of white wine.

"B'Sahtak!" He raised his glass. I clinked the beer bottle, sweaty in my hand, to his glass just as they did in western movies. I took a gulp and forced myself not to cough it out my nostrils.

He smiled at me, touched the young hairs of my beard softly. "You are the most beautiful man I've ever seen," he said.

I took another sip of my bitter beer.

"Are you hungry?"

I was famished, but I shook my head.

"For someone who writes such long emails, you sure don't say much," he joked. I tensed as he touched my waist.

"I'm not ticklish." I imitated a steady voice.

"Everyone is ticklish," he said, his hand wandering up to my ribs.

Suddenly I exploded with laughter. Through giggles I pleaded with him to stop, but he kept tickling. Then, when we were face to face, he kissed me on the lips. I froze at first. But then I grabbed him by the shoulders and brought him closer. His warm breath down my neck felt nice. I anchored his neck with my palm and slipped my fingers below the collar of his shirt. This was my first kiss.

"Okay, are you relaxed now?" he asked, breathless and pulling away.

"Why did you stop? Am I not doing it right?"

"You silly thing," he said, "it was great. But let's have dinner and talk first."

Adnan made us homemade burgers and fried some chips. As we ate at the dining room table he told me about his love of cars, showing me the pictures of his favourite Mercedes model that he kept in a booklet filled with cut-outs from foreign car magazines. I was attracted to the passion in his voice and comforted by the gentle way he explained things to me.

When I excused myself and went to the bathroom, I noticed squares on the hallway walls that suggested picture frames had been taken down. I opened the first door off the hall, but it was a bedroom, with a king-size bed covered in throw pillows, soft light showering the room in warmth. I clicked the door shut gently and found the bathroom next to it. Once inside, I snooped through the drawers and found a box of tampons underneath bandages and backup soaps. "You're married?" I asked Adnan when I returned to the living room.

"Yes," he said, without hesitation.

Adnan explained that he'd married a woman chosen by his parents. After getting an engineering degree in the U.S., where he'd found himself a boyfriend and begun an openly gay life in an East Coast city, his family induced him to return by threatening to cut him off. His parents believed they could straighten him out, remind him of his Syrian heritage, and force him to remain a man. Adnan accepted his fate. He was faithful to his wife for years, but three children into their marriage he could no longer deny his attraction to men. At the moment his wife was visiting a cousin in another city for a few days.

"I hope you don't mind," he said. "I should have told you sooner."

"I don't," I said.

For the next two years Adnan and I saw each other once or twice a month, depending on his wife's travel schedule. He snuck me in and let me stay over on the nights when his wife wouldn't be returning. Through bribery and connections, he managed to get a satellite receiver and access to American channels I'd never seen before. We spent evenings watching *Queer as Folk* naked on the comfortable sofa, my head in his lap. No Arabic subtitles, just beautiful white men on television navigating Pittsburgh's gay scene. Sometimes we cuddled in his bed while I read him poetry by Nizar Qabbani or summarized the latest short story I'd written. He bought me clothes, books, shoes, movie tickets, a leather jacket, and expensive cologne. For my eighteenth birthday he booked us a three-day trip to Beirut, where we stayed at a fancy hotel overlooking the Mediterranean. It was my first trip outside of Syria.

One evening, while watching *Grease*, he asked if he could call me by a different name. We were on the sofa facing each other, our legs interlaced.

"Ahmad is such a common name. Everyone's name is Ahmad." He paused the movie.

"What do you want to call me, then?"

"How about Danny? Like Danny Zuko." He pointed at John Travolta's young face, paused on the screen. "You look like him. And you even have the leather jacket."

73

I looked at Travolta on the screen, sceptical. "He's way more handsome than me."

"You silly thing," he said. "You are the most handsome man I've ever seen."

My relationship with Adnan would end soon. An Egyptian publisher had found my work in the YA forum online and been so impressed that they offered to release my first collection of short stories and briefly tour me through Egypt. The trip that was meant to last a couple of weeks ended with a job offer from a children's magazine in Cairo. I accepted it and returned to Damascus to say goodbye to friends.

Adnan's wife was in town at the time, so he couldn't offer his home for a final goodbye. Instead, he came to meet me at Al-Nofara café, right outside the doors of the Umayyad Mosque.

"If you ever return to Damascus, seek me out," he said. I squeezed his hand under the table.

Adnan and I were never together in the traditional sense of the word. He was never my boyfriend or partner. We never exchanged promise rings or spoke of commitment; we were both free to see other people. When I tell friends about Adnan, some laugh and cast him as my sugar daddy. Maybe our relationship was indeed transactional—he did offer me a lot of financial help and support—but he also offered me a sense of belonging. He was instrumental in ensuring I was armed with knowledge about who I was and what it meant to be a queer Syrian man. To this day, "you silly thing" is my favourite term of endearment for friends and lovers. He gave me much more than my name.

Coming out of the closet is overrated. We as a community put so much pressure on ourselves and on one another to come out, as if you're not officially queer until you've had that awkward conversation with your parents. The Western version of coming out is almost trivial in its simplicity. A child brings the topic of their sexuality to the dinner table. The family either accepts the child and asks them to pass the salt or rejects the child and flips the table. Either everyone is happy or everyone is miserable. Then, that's it! You've come out. You're done. Welcome to the club. Here's your complimentary bottle of glitter.

The problem with this approach is that it depends on acceptance from others. Placing such importance on the response from your blood family puts the power in their hands and takes it out of yours. And the effects of being rejected by them, especially at a young age, can be isolating, traumatic, and long-lasting.

Here, let me offer an alternative: Do your sexual preferences or gender representation run counter to the dictates of the dominant culture? Great! You are queer. There is no second step. You've made it, kid. What a joy!

There's no need for you to stand up to your conservative or religious family, put yourself in both physical and emotional danger, or risk losing connections with dear relatives. If you want to come out of the closet, that's fab. But if you want to stay in, that's valid, too.

Also, any queer person will tell you that coming out is never a one-and-done deal. I do it on a daily basis. In a restaurant when the bill comes or at a hotel checking in. It can be a passing matter, like referring to a husband, or it can turn into a full ordeal, like trying to book a wedding venue and having to repeatedly correct the heteronormative assumptions of the receptionist.

All of this is to say: I didn't need to come out to my family in order to accept myself. I thought I did. I believed it back when I was younger. I don't believe it anymore.

I'm stalling. I'm running in circles around the memory, avoiding it by any means necessary. I am doing the writer's acrobatics: my coming out story is on the horizon, but first let's look at this tertiary character, let's reminisce about that aspect of Damascus, let's philosophize the whole thing for a bit here. The memory of this moment from twenty years ago is faded, but it's also warped by the exaggerations of my teenage self, who fictionalized it, and of my twentysomething self, who downplayed it.

The memory is dead, but like an archaeologist I dig it out, brush the dust off its sharp edges, and analyze its contours under a magnifying glass.

⬤

It had been months since my midnight conversation with my father when I'd asked him to divorce my mother.

He'd promised to end the marriage and I believed him. But he was quick to return to his old habits, disappearing for weeks and dropping by only when it suited him. Meanwhile, my mother remained a frenzied force in our lives. Sometimes her pain was internal, a roaring beast that ate her from within and left her a shadow of a woman, barely able to navigate her way to the washroom. Sometimes it was external, a chaotic goddess casting her children away, leaving marks on my shoulder and upper back. I spent as much time as possible away from home—at the internet café, at Adnan's apartment, on the couches of friends I'd made through my online writing circles.

The night of my coming out was unplanned. Past midnight, I climbed the many stairs to our building and quietly slipped through the gate. In the living room, lit by the light of the television, my father sat waiting for me. My mother and sisters were asleep. He scolded me and asked where I'd been. I ignored him, went to my room, and closed the door behind me. Moments later he opened the door and ordered me to make him food.

I sighed, got up, and went to the kitchen, tiptoeing so as not to wake the others. I rummaged through the fridge and found some ghee, a sad-looking tomato, some pickles, and two eggs. I quickly fixed him an omelette, sliced the tomato and salted it. We were out of bread.

Silently, I brought the food tray to the living room, set it in front of my father, and turned to go back to my room.

"What is this?" he asked. "This is barely enough for two mouthfuls."

"It's all we have."

"That's a dinner you make for your father?"

"What do you want me to do?"

"The house is always dirty, the laundry is never clean, and this is the dinner you make me after a long day at work?" he shouted. I could hear one of my sisters rustle in her bed.

"And this is my responsibility?" I said calmly.

"Who else's should it be?"

For a moment I was quiet. I stood, looking him in the eyes, waiting for him to see the absurdity of the whole situation. Anger gathered in my chest.

All around me were images of how parents and households ought to be. Fathers with steady jobs and wise words, mothers who were soft and caring, homes that were kept beautiful and clean. Even at Adnan's I saw the touches his wife made to the house, the neat and tidy room his twelve-year-old son had, the cooked meals sitting in the fridge in glass containers, the fluffed pillows, the bookshelves. Inside I simmered with envy for them, and for the friends and cousins who seemed to have it all.

I also still believed on some level that my homosexuality, while unchangeable and outside my control, was inherently wrong. I saw it as the result of the traumatic experiences of my childhood. In my teenage logic, it was my mother's many abuses that had turned me off womankind altogether, and my father's absence that had made me into the soft feminine person I'd become. My parents had made me into an unlovable, disfigured creature. I fought this metamorphosis with all my might; I acted tough, worked out, smoked cigarettes, cursed. I stamped out my feminine side to please parents who were by turns abusive and neglectful.

Our imam claimed that homosexuality was a test from Allah: a way for God to see whether a person would stray or remain faithful and pure. Since I had failed this test, I saw myself as corrupted. Even though I'd begun to explore my sexuality, and had found solace in encounters with other queer folks, I was still years away from fully accepting it.

And the person I blamed for all of this was demanding a better dinner.

The conversation that followed is a blur. It was as if a demon possessed my body. I shouted curse words at my father. I kicked the table and sent food flying everywhere. I screamed like a tortured soul. I heard my sisters crying in the next room, but I didn't care. I barked and yelled and cried. My father tried to grab my shoulders, but I pushed him back. I told him to fuck off with his entitled demands. I asked him why I should prepare his food when he was never around to buy it. I told him I didn't know how to run a washing machine even if I wanted to, and that I didn't know how to raise his daughters for him.

"Stop. Enough," he said.

He'd left me alone with an abusive mother. I had to wear long-sleeve shirts to school, even on warm days, to hide her handprints on my arms. I had to beg relatives for pocket money and scraps of food. I had to carry the shame and embarrassment of our family around, seeing the looks in every neighbour's eye and hiding from men who'd loaned my father money.

"Ahmad! Enough!"

"You made this. You created it. You're supposed to be responsible for this. You're supposed to be a father!"

"Ahmad!"

"This life! This home! This family! You made all of this. This is all your fault."

"Ahmad!"

"You made me gay."

I wonder if you'd like a cut-and-dried ending to this conflict.

Would you like to hear the lurid details of what unfolded next? The screaming, the threats, the violence. The door slamming behind me, the clothes thrown from windows, the disownment.

In this narrative there's a hero and there's a villain. That's how conflict goes, right? My father, towering over me, threatening my life for my orientation. Me, a child of eighteen, risking it all for sexual liberation.

Alas, the story isn't that simple. The end of that fight stretched for months. Some days I was left alone and other days my father would follow me across Damascus, monitoring me. There were afternoons filled with loud shouting matches and evenings with slow and restrained conversations. Nights that I spent on my grandmother's couch and nights that I spent on the streets or with friends and distant relatives. The fight did not end abruptly. Even now, I don't know if it ever ended at all.

My father is not a villain. If anything, he lacks the charisma for it. He's a product of the Syrian society that taught him nothing about navigating his responsibilities.

Also, my father's villainy depends on who you're asking.

In his story, I'm the villain. I represent something that is considered evil by his family, society, laws of the land, religion, and everything in between. If my father were the one writing these pages I'd be depicted as a terrible son, a deviant entity, an abnormality that cost him dearly.

My connection to my family was and will always be complicated. It pulls and pushes and draws lines and breaks boundaries. That's the reality of being born into a society built on honouring sacred blood relationships and on burning bridges with those who stray.

I broke away from my family and became a free agent. I gained autonomy over my own destiny and was free to do what I wanted. That freedom wasn't given, it was taken by force.

The truth is, I sometimes regret coming out of the closet. I sometimes wonder, as I did after that conversation at Starbucks, if that alternate-reality Ahmad would have been a happier version than Danny. I was immature when I came out, propelled by anger rather than pride. It was a fight, and a silly one at that.

I remind myself in these low moments that my horizons broadened immeasurably because of that probable mistake, and that my rebellious teenage angst is why I'm capable of putting these words on a page today.

Weeks after my last fight with my father, he moved my sisters to my grandmother's home. He filed for divorce, stating unbearable living circumstances and my mother's mental health as reasons for the separation. The term "crazy" was used on the official divorce papers. The divorce wouldn't be finalized for another two years. My mother's family did not want to care for her. They had problems of their own, they claimed. They couldn't afford her moving back with them, they insisted. They bickered over who would get to keep my parents' home. My father remarried a woman six months older than me and rented an apartment for his new wife and my sisters.

That's when it was official: I no longer had a home.

FAMILY

It was dark in the cinema. The same movies had been playing since the late seventies, their reels old and crackling, the images onscreen robotic and scratchy. The male stars distanced themselves from these films after their release, while the women lost their careers altogether in the hard societal turn toward Islamic conservatism of the 1980s.

You could call it soft-core porn: clumsily plotted stories of kidnapped women who'd do anything to be released, or of righteous men steered toward sin. Syrian actresses gave up their birth names and took on suggestive pseudonyms—Ighraa (Temptation) and Nashwa (Pleasure)—baring it all for the camera. Syrian actors with hairy chests and skimpy swimming shorts grabbed and kissed the women, tracing hands down their bodies and gyrating against them.

Posters on the cinema's glass doors showcased the sexy scenes and offered two movies for the price of one. You could slip in at any hour of the day and find a number of men, lonely in their seats, watching the movies for hours. Waiting.

I paid little attention to what was happening onscreen as I shuffled in, welcomed by the smell of stale cigarettes. Heads turned at the sound of the door closing behind me. I walked down the aisle to the front row, then turned around and slowly walked back up until I locked eyes with one of the men and made my way to the wooden chair next to him. We silently watched the movie for a bit, his knee brushing against mine. Then his hand caressed my thigh and his fingers found their way to my jeans' buttons. He unbuckled my belt and grabbed my dick in his cold palm. Neither of us took our eyes off the screen while he massaged my penis. I heard him sigh, a controlled exhale so as not to be heard. I leaned back in my seat, slid down slightly, and extended a hand to his side. His penis was already hard and sticking out of his fly. We jerked each other off while the actors onscreen undressed and skinny-dipped in a river.

"To the bathroom, milkmen!" someone shouted from the back of the theatre. This was a coded line yelled at intervals by theatre staff, who urged men to finish the job in the bathrooms rather than leave a sticky mess for them to mop up.

Soon the credits were rolling, leaving the hall in almost total darkness. A moan came from another corner and was quickly interrupted. The man next to me took the chance, lifted the armrest between us, and dipped his head in my lap. Blood gathered in my face as I heard him slurp between my thighs. I quickened my strokes of his penis, but he pushed my hand away and jerked himself off, pointing his penis away from his clothes. Soon I ejaculated in his mouth; his body twitched as he finished on the floor.

He wiped his mouth on the shoulder of his jacket and looked up. Another movie began to play, bringing a dim light into the theatre. I saw his face clearly for the first time: he was in his late twenties with a day worker's tan and a guilty look in his eyes. He avoided my gaze, fixed his clothes, and rushed to the door without another word.

I buckled my pants and headed out into the afternoon sun. Then I found a corner across from the cinema, pulled out my pack of cheap cigarettes, and lit a match.

I was empty. The encounter barely lingered in my mind before slowly flickering away as if it had never happened. I was already considering heading back into the cinema after my cigarette. There was an ache in my chest. Was it loneliness? A lack of intimacy? A need to feel desired? I wasn't sure.

I'd been living on my own for over a year, renting a room in a shared home in old Damascus, close to the bridge that had been built upon the house where I was born. I continued to work at the internet café and had gotten into a two-year diploma program in English Literature and Translation at the University of Damascus.

Taking a drag of my cigarette, I mentally counted the liras in my wallet and wondered if I had enough to splurge on a shawarma sandwich.

That's when I saw her.

She waved to the men who worked at the cinema as she stepped out into the sunlight, sauntering in her tight jeans and a loose blouse that showed her bra straps. An old woman in a white hijab and long jacket flashed her a dirty look. She fished into her cleavage, pulled out a crumpled ball of money, then smoothed it on her thigh, counting openly in front of all who passed. Satisfied, she stuffed the bills into a men's wallet from her back pocket. Our eyes locked. She smiled; I averted my gaze, pretending to look at shoes in the shop across the street.

"What are you looking at, gorgeous?" she said. I continued my charade. "Won't you talk to me then?"

I pointed at myself. "Me?"

"I've seen you around here before," she mused. "What's your name, honey?"

"I think you're mistaking me for someone else." I turned away.

"Wait! I don't bite," she called. I felt embarrassed. People had started to look at us, and I didn't want to make a scene.

"How can I help you?"

"Okay, tough guy. I just wanted to say hello. My name's Sama. What's yours?"

"Danny."

"Like Daniel the prophet?" She looked me up and down. "You don't look Jewish." Apparently Danny was a common name among the dwindling Jewish population of Damascus.

"What are you up to?" She sidled up to me and grabbed my arm. Up close I could see how tall she was. "You want to get a coffee or something to eat?"

"Lady, I don't think you—"

"We're just walking and talking, Danny."

I could tell from her accent that she wasn't from Damascus. Maybe from Northern Syria, or even Iraq. We walked for an hour, and Sama did most of the talking. She waved to the people working in cafés and ice cream parlours, at jewellers and clothing boutiques. When we got to the shawarma place, she bought us each a sandwich. The chef standing in front of the oven, twirling the meat, greeted her warmly.

"Who's the guy?" he asked, eyeing me.

"New on the market." She winked.

We continued our aimless walk while Sama spoke of mundane things: her love of stray cats, her favourite shop to buy makeup from. She was older than me, maybe in her mid-thirties. Her long hair was tied up in a ponytail and sharp, majestic cheekbones anchored her face. She'd outlined her big, rosy lips with black. Like me, she had a small birthmark on her right cheek, which endeared me to her.

Sunset came, and with it a light drizzle of rain. Sama invited me over to her place.

"Listen, I think you have the wrong—"

"Oh, shush. I know you're not interested in my kind."

"What do you mean?"

"Child, I picked you up outside the old cinema. We both know what I mean."

"I'm not—" My face burned.

"Just come," she said, her smile genuine, almost angelic. "You'll be safe there."

I gave in. We boarded a bus to the outskirts of eastern Damascus. I watched the cityscape morph from tall, clean buildings to new structures hastily built—cracked walls, misaligned windows. Courtyards meant to house fountains were instead filled with dirt and tangled webs of electrical wires.

Finally we made it to Sama's: a humble apartment on the third floor of a building with mouldy walls. It was humid as we entered and climbed the stairs.

"Mother! You're home!" A woman appeared and quickly tightened her blouse across her chest when she saw me. "You didn't say you were bringing company."

Over the next couple of hours more people arrived. Men we'd seen at the cafés and jewellers, even the chef from the shawarma shop. They showed up in groups of twos or threes and walked in as if they owned the place; some even had keys. They kissed Sama on the cheek and then Sawsan, the woman I'd met at the door. The boys lounged comfortably on the sofas, resting their heads in one another's laps. Their voices got an octave or two higher. One of them referred to himself by a woman's name, and everyone laughed. Most of them were in their early twenties, but later in the night four other men in their forties showed up.

The chef introduced himself as Omar. He had freckles on his cheeks and large black eyes. "That's Amjad," he said, pointing, "and that's Mohammed, but don't call him that. He goes by Mark because he thinks he looks like that American actor."

"Wahlberg?" I asked, incredulous. We laughed.

"Over there is Hassan," he said, pointing to the most flamboyant of the bunch, "but we call her Hasnah in the Jaoo."

"In the what?" *Jaoo*, which in Arabic translates to environment or weather, didn't make sense to me in this context.

"Ah. You are brand new! Jaoo is our code word for the gay community in Damascus."

Omar explained that in Syria the community is broken into a system of family trees. Each individual belongs to a family with chosen siblings and a hierarchical mother. In this case Sama was the mother and the five others were her chosen daughters. Each daughter was in turn allowed to bring in their own chosen children, creating a family tree with granddaughters, cousins, nephews, and nieces. Everyone was free to choose the gender pronouns they felt comfortable with, although they all knew that such a freedom dissolved outside the safety of this home.

"Sama has siblings from when she was younger," Omar said. "But now she has family of her own."

"Why would she do that?" I asked.

"What? Leave her original family?"

"No. I mean why would a woman run a house for gay men?"

Omar looked at me. "You don't know?"

"Don't know what?"

Sama, who'd been eavesdropping on the conversation, leaned in and playfully whispered to me.

"Child. I'm trans."

◖

Sama would later tell me about her experience with top surgery and facial feminization, for which she paid a sympathetic local doctor in cash and was ushered into the back room of his clinic at a late hour of the night. She was frightened when she realized that the doctor was the only person there, surrounded by scary medical tools she could only just make out in the dim light. She asked him to stop when he administered the anaesthesia, but it was too late. She passed out and woke up alone hours later, swollen and covered in tight bandages. Her chest was bruised and her face was painful to the touch. Her recovery lasted months, prolonged by multiple infections and other unanticipated complications. She vowed never to go under the knife again.

"The doctor wanted to also do the bottom surgery, but I will never do that," Sama told me. She'd had enough pain and suffering, she explained, and wouldn't tempt fate again with a risky surgery under inexperienced hands.

"I'm reminded every day that I am not who I am supposed to be," she added. "But I'm not willing to lose my life for it."

Sama had studied to be a nurse back when she was presenting as male, but since then she couldn't find work in any hospital. Her Syrian ID listed her as male and revealed her deadname. She'd lived in the house of her chosen family for most of her early twenties. Then she leaned into sex work, starting small, conducting her business in empty parking lots or at the cinema where we'd met. Later she made the switch, renting her own apartment and asking other sex workers to join her.

Sama invited me to the parties she threw for her clients, filling the space with loud music, clouds of cigarette and hash smoke, and her put-on laugh. Men came in bearing food and drink; one after the other they'd slip into a bedroom with Sama or one of her girls, pay, and then leave.

"Aren't you afraid your clients will find out you're a trans woman?" I asked her once. "Are you worried for your safety?"

"It's all theatre, child," Sama said with a laugh. "I pretend I enjoy their company, and they pretend they can't see my penis."

In Sama's home, I flourished.

During the day I kept to myself, attending classes at the university and taking shifts at the internet café. In the evenings I showed up at Sama's and kissed her three times on the cheeks. Sometimes she made me her famous yalanji or her rich kibbeh. Other times Omar brought leftover chicken shawarma from his shop, or another sibling would show up with pastries from the café he worked at. We played cards, smoked argileh, and watched DVDs on the desktop computer we'd all pitched in to buy.

Eventually, Sama asked me about my own blood relatives.

"Dead," I lied. "My mother died when I was twelve, and my father died last year."

"Where do you live?" she said. "You can move in with us here if you want."

"I have a room in an old home in Damascus." I didn't want to leave that room, which reminded me of the home I was born into. Tired and dusty, with a wooden column in the middle carrying the weight of the old ceiling.

Later that week, Sama claimed me as a daughter. It was a controversial choice, as I was too young and new to the Jaoo. Many wanted the hierarchical power that came with the title, but Sama reminded them that she was the mother of the house and whatever she said was law.

On nights when Sama didn't have to work, we gathered in her home. The boys belly danced and the girls gossiped about the other queer families in our orbit: who slept with whom, who cheated on whom, who was forced by his parents to marry a woman—the usual. We smoked hash and watched soap operas until Sama told us to go to sleep so that we'd be rested for work and school the next day. I slept less and less in my own rented room, instead sharing a bed with two or three chosen siblings. Sometimes we snored so loud we kept one another awake. Other times we cuddled, whispered stories, and gossiped until dawn.

Under Sama there were five daughters: Omar and I, another

gay man I didn't get along with, Sawsan, and another trans woman. Under us were a number of nephews and nieces mainly mothered by the trans women; Omar and I didn't have offspring of our own. Male-identifying family members were given female names, either chosen by themselves or offered by others. Sama called me Labibah after a smart but condescending Arabic cartoon character.

It strikes me now how similar the family tree system in Damascus is to the underground queer communities in large Western cities across North America. I'm not sure how they evolved to be so alike. With the political firewall across Syria, we had very little contact with the outside world—we'd have enough trouble even learning about such a marginalized culture, let alone imitating it. And the family tree system in Syria is deeply rooted, existing in the region even before borderlines divided it into multiple countries. Sama, for instance, was able to trace her spiritual bloodline back to the early twenties. I wonder: Did the two systems grow, separately but similarly, in response to the universal needs of the community: to overcome trauma, to fulfil desires, to experience the acceptance of family?

The Jaoo had its own rules and regulations. Rarely did two gay men from the same family get together—it felt wrong, like sleeping with your sibling. Instead, we "married" outside the family. Such unions were celebrated with ceremonies and parties in isolated countryside villas. We developed our own language, similar to pig Latin, and peppered our public conversations with it. Sama visited her chosen mother—my grandmother—on a monthly basis. A gay man in his late sixties, he'd gather his daughters for a Friday brunch once a month. I met him twice, but he preferred to stick to those he took on as his daughters.

"Too many grandchildren," Sama told me. "He can't stand the blabber."

Omar, my chosen sibling, also became my best friend. He came to my work on his break, brought food, and spent the afternoon with me. Omar loved to draw, inspired by the comics we both adored. Together we hatched stories of time-travelling best friends who hop uncontrollably across eras. I wrote the storyboards and he drew the characters to look like us.

I tried to introduce Omar to Adnan, whom I'd been seeing for over a year by then. Adnan, however, preferred a more private and controlled environment; he didn't want to be part of the Jaoo.

"It's fun for a while," he said, head resting on my naked thigh. "Then suddenly half the city knows about you. These bitches don't know when to stop talking."

By the time I turned nineteen I'd found comfort I hadn't dreamt of merely two years before. Long gone were the days of neglectful and abusive parents. Now I had a chosen family that cared about me: siblings I could laugh uncontrollably with, a mother figure I could lean my head against, a father figure who protected me and worried for my future.

When the offer to publish my short stories in Egypt came along, my family did what families do: they supported me.

"You should go," Omar insisted.

"With what money? I don't even have a passport." I took a bite of the shawarma sandwich he'd brought me.

"You're an only male child. You won't face trouble getting your passport." He explained that the Syrian Army service, mandatory only for those with male siblings, wouldn't prohibit me from travelling outside the country.

Death and Other Fools came out in January 2003 at the Cairo International Book Fair. Sama, Omar, and my other siblings pooled together some extra cash for a return bus ticket so that I could attend the launch and the book tour.

At a Red Sea port I presented my new Syrian passport to the Egyptian border officer with both hands, like a prayer or a gift. He grabbed it, flipped its pages, stamped it, and tossed it back to me. I ran to the bus, relieved. When I arrived in Cairo I called Sama from the first pay phone I could find.

"This city is massive," I said. "I don't know anyone here."

"You're bigger than any city," she said. "You'll be able to make the best of this trip and return victorious to your mother's home."

◠

I have a few photos from that first trip to Egypt that I keep in an old album.

I barely fill the leather jacket Adnan gifted me. The thick hair I've since lost is sculpted with the gel Sama had recommended. Omar had contoured my fuzzy beard with a single blade. I stand in front of the Cairo Tower with a copy of the story collection in my hand. I'm smiling a genuine smile, as if I knew that this city would soon become my home, that it would devour me as I devoured it.

In another photograph I'm behind a table on a stage, the youngest on a panel of new authors presenting their work. Thin as I might have been, I looked alive. People asked me questions and the words just came. Interacting with the world as a writer felt so natural, like destiny. In yet another photo I'm in line for a massive roller coaster at Dream Park on the outskirts of Cairo, looking terrified. My publisher had asked what I wanted to do for fun while I was in Cairo. "I want to ride a roller coaster," I'd said. "We don't have any in Syria."

On my last day there I met Ahmed Khaled Tawfik, an Egyptian writer famous for the YA novels I'd been reading ever since I learned how. I was starstruck—he was the Stephen King of the region. We conversed for hours, then he recommended me to the editor of a local children's magazine. There was a job for me if I was ever to return to Cairo.

I wanted to return to Cairo.

"Don't you think the decision is a bit rushed?" Sama asked on our way back from the bus station in Damascus. Omar drove the rented car. Snow had gathered on the sidewalks, soon to melt away with the first rays of sun in the morning. "Maybe think about it? Consider your options first?"

"What future do I have here? My university diploma isn't worth the paper it was printed on! Am I going to work in an internet café for the rest of my life? Live in a shared home until my dying days?"

"Nothing wrong with a shared home with those you love, child."

"I didn't mean to offend, Mother," I said. "This is a gift, but my life can be much more than this over there."

"Let him go, Mother," Omar said. "If he's successful, we'll have a famed writer in our family. If he fails, he'll have a warm bed in our home."

On one of my last nights in Damascus, Sama, Omar, and the others took me out. We walked down to Bab Tuma and slipped through the old labyrinth as the light of day slowly died out, a spring chill filling the air. Churches lit up the Christian district; Latin and old Arabic hymns echoed across the cobblestone streets. Cars honked at our group, big enough to take over the two sidewalks and the road itself, and angry drivers cursed us. We found a café warm with candlelight and ordered manaqish and heavy tea and beer. Omar and I played tawleh on a mosaic-adorned backgammon set. Sama insisted on paying the bill, and no one could deny her whatever she wanted.

Outside again our eyes twinkled under orange streetlamps as I felt the weight of the historic homes leaning on one another, soon to be demolished for another bridge. I burrowed into Sama's side, and Omar put an arm around my shoulder.

We found an underground bar close to Bab Sharqi, strategically under-lit to afford discretion for those wishing to escape the eyes of society. We ordered more beers and cocktails. Then the music came, and we danced. Sama held my face between her palms and kissed me on the nose. Omar hugged me a moment too long. Others joked that I was like a May windstorm that arrived without warning, ruffled everyone's feathers, and left as quickly as it appeared.

At four in the morning, we walked the silent city. Streets that were too crowded in the morning were now empty of souls. The dome over Hamidiyah market—covering us like a tunnel—had little holes across its metal expanse, and through them we could see the stars. Or at least we thought we could.

Drunk, we sang a Fairuz song, off-key and with little fidelity to the actual lyrics. In a whisper at first, then loud enough to be heard across the whole empty economic district.

The song, filled with the duty of departure and the surrender to goodbyes, made me cry. Sama, alcohol on her breath, hugged me and joined me in tears. The others huddled around us as she pulled me close to her chest. In the distance, we heard the call for the morning prayers.

CLOSETS

At ten in the evening on New Year's Eve 2005, I was already tipsy.

The car sped along a dark highway. The driver, a young Egyptian man with thick hair and soft features, kept skipping songs, unable to decide what tune he wanted to drive to. We were seven in a car meant for five. Most of the passengers were Egyptian, except for me and a random white American working at a local NGO. Shiraz, the only woman in the group, sat on my lap in the front seat.

"Are we there yet?" Shiraz asked, that age-old question.

"Another half an hour at least," the driver said.

Shiraz was petite, but what she lacked in stature she made up for in personality: loud when she laughed, sexually suggestive when she joked, and intense when she angered. She'd found her spiritual family among gay Egyptian men and had instantly taken a liking to me. We liked to argue about the political climates in both Syria and Egypt, making grand statements as if we, at the tender age of twenty-two, had all the knowledge we needed about the world.

"Who'll be the biggest whore tonight?" one of the four men asked from the back, and the driver lowered the volume. Slowly I realized that all eyes were on me.

"Oh, come on," I said.

"Danny, you're always the biggest slut at these parties," Shiraz said. "How many people will you make out with tonight? Six? Seven?"

I scoffed, and everyone laughed. "I bet you'll break your own record," she continued. "I bet you'll make out with at least twelve people tonight."

"You know what?" I said. "I'll take that bet. I'll even count them for you."

The car roared with laughter, swallowed by the dark highway around us, then silence returned. Again we heard the first thirty seconds of a song, interrupted by the driver skipping to the next.

The road felt abandoned of cars, and with the Egyptian desert stretching out on both sides, we had only our headlights to guide us. The party organizer, a gay man we all knew, had rented a secluded villa for the festivities. He ran these kinds of underground events all the time: Halloween bashes in cavernous clubs, trivia nights in his penthouse, an impromptu orgy to which only a select few were invited. He paid the right people the right amount of money to make sure we were never bothered by the authorities. We'd each shelled out an exorbitant sum to get our code name on the New Year's Eve party guest list and were promised a gay old time.

When we arrived the villa was showered in sparkling lights. Inside, a VIP area had been cordoned off, but we couldn't afford entry. Outside was a pool filled with foam, an LED-illuminated dance floor, and a cash bar. We huddled at the end of the outdoor line in the cool breeze of an Egyptian winter.

"Only men allowed," the bouncer said when we reached him, singling out Shiraz.

She already paid for the ticket, we argued, and no one had told us the party was limited to men. If she couldn't go in, none of us would. It wasn't as though she could call a cab to take her home. Finally the bouncer sighed and let us all in.

We were welcomed by the beats of the Black Eyed Peas. The party had been going on for an hour or so, with most people still standing in corners chitchatting. The dance floor was still empty; foam had gathered leisurely over the pool's calm surface. The sky, dark and starless, reflected the projectors' lights back at us. Someone handed me a fruity drink and another waved at me from afar. Slowly the group I came with dispersed, each finding their own tribe.

I danced with someone I barely knew, then he introduced me to his shirtless friend, who looked dazed. He gave me a hug and rested his head on my shoulder. As I untangled myself he leaned in for a kiss. I made out with him, tasting the alcohol on his breath, before he slipped away. Then I ran into someone else I knew. Shorter than me, bald, green eyes that I was pretty sure were contacts.

"Hey . . ." I trailed off, unsure of his name.

"Hey, you," he said, clearly just as lost.

"Are you here on your own?"

"No. I have—"

I didn't give him a chance to talk. I grabbed him close and made out with him, too. He relaxed in my arms. I caressed his neck as we kissed, then rested my palm on the small of his back. A moment later, we separated.

"That was unexpected," he whispered.

"Yeah. See you soon." I walked away.

Two, I counted in my head. *That's two.* Shiraz stood alone in the middle of the yard, nursing a drink. In the distance I saw someone else I knew. I rushed over, already preparing to add them to my list.

A while later I found my way to Shiraz. She stood where I'd left her, looking around at the sea of shirtless men who'd taken over the dance floor. Foam floated off the tanned, smooth bodies of gay Egyptian men as they got in and out of the pool.

"That's twelve," I told Shiraz, proud of my accomplishment.

"Twelve what?"

I realized in that moment how stupid I sounded. "Never mind. How's your night?"

Shiraz must have answered, but I wasn't listening. I had a couple more drinks, and someone handed me a lit joint that I inhaled twice, holding it between my thumb and pointer. I was stoned and drunk, but I was also high on the fact that I felt desirable, worthy of love. All these eager men kissed me and relaxed in my arms. They picked me. I was so joyful, I was jittery.

Midnight came. We counted down, and I made out with the first man I found in front of me. We shouted in joy welcoming the new year, then passed two hours on the dance floor.

Suddenly, around two in the morning, all the lights in the villa went off. The music died, the sprinkled lights wheezed and darkened, and silence descended. Then the whispers began to circulate. *The police are here. We'll be arrested.* I didn't know where the exit was. Heck, I didn't even know where my shirt was. The crowd of sweaty bodies around me opened; people scattered. I panicked. I mentally scrolled through the list of lies I could tell the officers: *I didn't know this was a gay party, I was just in the neighbourhood, I don't speak Arabic.* They all sounded dumb in my head.

"Everyone, calm down," a megaphoned voice intoned. "The electricity is out. There is a generator, but it needs ten minutes to kick in."

Sighs of relief could be heard. Soon enough, the darkened bodies returned to crowd me. When someone felt me up from behind I turned around and made out the shape of my green-eyed friend.

"Oh, hey you."

Without saying a word he got down on his knees and took my dick in his mouth. Then, when a stranger cozied up behind me, I rested my body against him. His breath was warm on my neck and I felt his naked torso pressed to my back. Around us, many others took advantage of the dark. Within seconds the yard was emptied of talk then filled with hushed gasps and short giggles. When my eyes adjusted to the darkness, all I could see around me were bodies entwined.

Eventually the lights flickered on and the music returned. I quickly buckled my jeans. The three of us blinked in the light, then laughed.

Then I saw Shiraz, a drink in her hand and tears in her eyes.

"What's wrong?" I was quick to take her in my arms. She snuggled into me, unbothered by my sweat.

"It was dark, and I was alone," she said softly. "I was afraid we were all going to be arrested."

She shivered. I held her close and murmured that it would be okay. That I was there. That everything was going to be fine.

"Midnight came and no one kissed me, Danny."

"Well, you're surrounded by gay men, you silly thing," I joked.

"It's not funny," she protested. Her eyes met mine, and in my haze they seemed to glow. Maybe it was the sparkling lights, the tears still hanging. Maybe I was high and drunk and didn't know better. But in that moment I found within her the same fire that had been burning in me since childhood. We were loved only when we were desired. We both ached from the same wound; we both wanted to be reminded that we mattered. We'd never known what it meant to be worthy, only what it meant to be wanted. Yet on that night, while I'd been filled to the brim with desirability, Shiraz had faced rejection from every corner, witnessing everyone else's wildest cravings on display.

So I did what I thought I should do. I kissed her.

She kissed me deeper and we embraced, pulling each other close. Shiraz guided my hand up her shirt, to her breast. I quickly snapped it back, and in my drunken and dazed stupor said the first thing that came to mind.

"Eww."

"What?" She pulled back, crossing her arms over her chest.

"No. I mean—" I stumbled. "Shiraz, I'm gay."

"I know that." She turned and ran away. I stood like an idiot and watched her get the car keys from our driver and rush past the bored bouncer. *I should follow her*, I thought. *I should apologize.*

But just as I approached the exit, I was startled by a familiar face.

"Ahmad?" It was Mohammed, one of my coworkers from the magazine. "Is that you?"

In my early years in Egypt, my life had to be compartmentalized.

Nine to five, I was an editor and an in-house writer at a major children's magazine in Cairo. My best friends were the group of writers and readers I met on the magazine's online forum. I attended panels and readings and hosted my own events. I wore neutral-toned shirts and silver-rimmed glasses, and I carried a handbag filled with papers and a heavy laptop. My friends called me Ahmad.

But after six, I was a gay man. I met my people on sites like Gaydar and Manjam. We hung out in my apartment until the late hours, drinking beer and smoking hashish. I had unprotected sex with handsome Egyptian men and foreigners mesmerized by Cairo's lights. I gambled away caution for joy; risky behaviour became my norm. I wore torn jeans and loud T-shirts, spiked my hair with gel, and made sure I always had sexy underwear on. My friends called me Danny.

I believed that the two lives would not intersect, that I could successfully maintain both personas as long as I kept them separate. I thought of it less as a double life and more as two half-lives, constantly at odds with each other. Choosing to live fully as Danny would have meant a life on the margins, perpetual fear of police harassment, and limited job prospects. Choosing to live fully as Ahmad would have been to deny an essential part of me, to leave myself open to matchmaking setups and the pressure to propose, take a bride.

In the homophobic climate of Egypt at the time, Ahmad was a necessary disguise. Just a few years earlier, in 2001, fifty-two gay men had been arrested in Cairo on a moored Nile cruiser that doubled as a gay night club. Egyptian authorities apprehended them in the early hours of the morning, paraded them across town in police cars, then threw them into two cells without beds for five months.

Fifty of the men were charged with habitual debauchery and obscene behaviour, while two were charged with contempt for religion. They all pleaded innocent.

After years of trials and retrials and mistrials, a media circus and an intense global outrage, the men were finally handed their sentences: twenty-one received three years in hard labour prisons, and twenty-nine were acquitted. The judge—known only by his last name, Abdel Karim—was rumoured to have been bribed. Those whose families paid the right price were released, and those who couldn't afford it—or whose families refused to pay for their child's freedom owing to the shame of their actions—were handed jail time.

In that ever-sunny city, then, I couldn't lead a singular life. The only way to survive was to become two people in one body. Like a werewolf, I was just another face in the crowd in the daytime and a menace after dark. The blending of my two sides calmed me down, soothed my burning with ice. It meant I could have it all in a city I loved.

Cairo is a metropolis that knows no silence. The call to prayer echoes from the capital's mosques five times a day, and at night the city roars with the sounds of cars and trains and subways. I was in awe of the pyramids of Giza, the majestic Nile cleaving the city in two, the fast, unlimited internet. I was enchanted by its many bridges, built in the sixties and early seventies as a sign of wealth and prosperity. My long-running fixation on bridges, both literal and figurative, began there.

Most of all, I was in awe of how many more books I had access to and how many readers I could reach. Cairo is the capital of literature in the Arab world. Its writers are well known across all twenty-five Arabic-speaking countries, and its magazines are widely published across the region. If you wanted to make it as an Arab author, this city was the place to be.

During my first year in Cairo, I read dozens of books that gathered in an ever-growing pile in my home, and I dedicated most of my time and energy to writing. My fiction, children's stories, and columns were published in multiple local newspapers and magazines. At the same time I had inserted myself into a tight-knit group of gay men and was exploring the city's underground queer community. Cairo is a city of boys. Clustered together on street corners and at cafés and theatres and fast-food joints, playing pranks and being loud, smoking their shishas and drinking their beers—the Cairo queers had no choice but to imitate their heterosexual counterparts. We hid Shiraz between us like a dirty secret and acted as the straights did, if you don't count the gay sex (which straight men had only *some* of the time).

Cairo is so big, I mused back then; I was happy to disappear into a city of millions, to become but one of its many boys. How would anyone ever recognize my daytime self through their evening eyes?

So when I stood stunned in front of a colleague in the middle of a gay New Year's Eve party, morning came crashing right into night.

◗

I could see in the distance that Shiraz had gotten into the car. I worried she might drive away, abandon us in the middle of nowhere. The music echoed in my head and lights flickered around me.

I greeted my colleague. "Oh, hey Mohammed."

"Call me Moe," he said. "What are you doing here?"

Ah. Moe. A fellow separator of identities.

"I could ask you the same question," I said. Shiraz turned the car on, and the headlights beamed.

"Are you a khawal?"

I cringed at the word, the Arabic equivalent of *faggot*. It felt as though a bucket of ice water had been dropped on me. "Why would you call me that?"

"Who are we kidding, Ahmad?" he said.

"Call me Danny."

Moe was older than me, maybe in his early thirties. He was handsome, tall, and lean, with clear olive skin. You could see his wealth in his fancy car, designer sunglasses, straight teeth. At work he kept to the other dozen or so other rich guys, nearly identical to him in their preferences. His own little gang.

"I have to go," I said, gesturing to the car. "See you in the office, Moe."

He flashed me a fake smile, and I walked to the car. The doors were locked. I looked at Shiraz behind the wheel. *"Really?"* I mouthed. She sank into the driver's seat and clicked the unlock button. I got in.

"I am so sorry," I said.

"That was not cool, Danny."

"I know."

We sat in silence while the party continued in front of us, lights flickering, music seeping in through the car windows. It was early morning now and people were leaving, cars filling with friends or strangers who'd just met.

"I ran into someone from work," I said. "I don't think he likes me very much."

"Why?"

"He called me a khawal."

"But you are a khawal," she teased.

I giggled and elbowed her softly. "I don't think he meant it like that."

She sighed and turned on the radio; Umm Kulthum was singing about being so drunk in love that you'd run in joy so fast you'd catch up to your own shadow. The driver soon arrived, accompanied by a friend. We'd lost three of our companions to other rides. Shiraz agreed to drive, since she'd had the least to drink. As we were about to leave I saw the bald green-eyed man standing by the gate.

I rolled down my window. "Want a ride?" He came over and got in.

"Really?" the driver protested from the backseat, squeezed into the middle.

"Sorry, girl," I said. "I can't help myself."

◠

A week or so later I was entering the break room when Moe and his circle of friends laughed. He shushed them, but they followed me with their eyes. Soon after, the illustrator I collaborated with on a series of sci-fi comics requested a change of assignment. The forty-something content creator stopped saying good morning to me and kept our conversations clipped. The young and inexperienced hijabi woman I shared an office with started playing Quran recordings throughout the day instead of her usual Amr Diab songs. In my desk drawer I found a booklet on how to resolve my relationship with Allah. On the inside of a bathroom stall appeared a pencil drawing of an erect penis and a written suggestion to get in touch with Danny if you fancy your cock sucked.

I kept my head down, ignored the signs. *It's a storm*, I told myself. *It will pass soon, and everyone will forget.* I breezed through the stares and the jokes. I pretended I didn't hear the giggles. My balancing act had failed; my foot had slipped off the tightrope and I was falling. Midair, I pretended it was all just fine.

One day about a month into the new year, I arrived at the office to find that my desktop computer was no longer password-protected and all of my browsing history had been deleted. I was instructed to meet with Human Resources and the executive manager of the magazine.

"Some rumours regarding you have come to our attention, Ahmad," the HR woman said. Behind her, the manager and a security guard avoided my gaze.

"Your personal life is none of our business," she said. "But we have some concerns about the safety and security of this office."

"I'm not sure what this is about," I lied.

"Well, we want to ask you some direct questions," the woman continued. The manager kept silent while the guard shifted uncomfortably in his seat. "Your honesty and cooperation will determine your future in this company."

The HR woman exchanged a meaningful look with the manager, who nodded soberly. She shuffled the papers on her desk and cleared her throat.

"Do you have AIDS?"

At the time, even just getting tested for HIV was seen as an admission of homosexuality. Most gay men I knew back in Syria and here in Cairo refused to take the test, and I had followed suit. We feared being exposed to the authorities, regardless of the result.

Her blunt question threw me off. I had planned on denying being gay, if asked. I planned to get mad, to exhale through my nostrils like a bull. I would blame bored coworkers with nothing better to do and show them photos of Shiraz, claiming she was my girlfriend. But this I wasn't prepared for.

"I don't know," I said.

A victorious smile cracked on the manager's face. "A man with a clean past would know he doesn't have AIDS," he said.

"We've booked an appointment for you today in a private lab nearby," the HR woman said. "The guard will accompany you from now until we learn the results."

"I don't think—"

"It's either that or you lose your job, effective immediately."

There was no more pretense. I stood up in the silent room and walked out the door. The security guard followed. In the rest of the office, laughter and chatter emanated from the cubicles. My jacket was still at my desk, but I had no desire to be paraded over to get it. Instead I headed to the elevator.

At least I'll know my status, I thought *This is a good thing*. But my face in the elevator mirror didn't seem convinced. I wouldn't call myself a pillar of sexual health. I had repeatedly placed myself in high-risk situations: unprotected sexual encounters, conducted under a haze of drugs and alcohol.

We walked to the lab, where we were ushered into a backroom. A technician drew my blood under the watchful eyes of the guard. We were asked to remain seated there for the next couple of hours. The guard sat across the room from me, listening to recordings of the Quran on his MP3 player, loud enough that I could hear the words through his headphones.

Thoughts crowded my mind, as if rushing to exit a building on fire. *Will I lose my job? How will I pay rent? Will the Egyptians send me back to Syria? Will the police be called? On what charges?* I teared up in my seat, and the guard saw me. He ignored me still.

By the afternoon, we were informed of my negative results. When I returned to the office, my belongings had been gathered into a garbage bag on my desk, next to an envelope containing my last paycheque. The lobby, usually a bustling hub, was strangely empty. The security guard accompanied me back out to the street, then finally let me go.

I struggle with the decision to tell you this story. Lateral violence in marginalized communities is not a topic I want to approach lightly. Did Moe know what he was doing when he outed me to his friends? Did he expect the story to explode within the office or lead to where it led? Was it a self-defence mechanism, outing me before I had the chance to out him? Was this some kind of ugly, twisted jungle law— out or be outed?

Or maybe it was simply internalized homophobia. He saw himself as anything but a khawal, with his perfect life and unmistakable masculinity and prized fiancée. Danny, on the other hand, was the khawal, with his femme friends and soft-spoken manners and poetic writing. We had never shared a sky, Moe and me. We'd never had the same prayers. Possibly, Moe never felt that he was destroying the life of a fellow queer man, because he himself never connected with that identity outside a buried sexual desire. Perhaps he'd drunk from the same poisoned well his society was built upon. Did he hate himself and, by extension, me?

The rumour spread beyond the office, seeping into conversations among writers and readers, both in real life and online. The stories were elaborated upon and expanded. My sex life became a topic of speculation in private settings and on public forums. A writer I respected was heard saying in a café that I played the homosexual card as an attention-seeking game, hoping to come off as eccentric or edgy.

My job applications were rejected, sometimes within moments of submitting them. Days of job searching stretched into weeks as I scoured the postings for every magazine and newspaper in Cairo. I had one freelancing gig—with the managing editor of a Saudi children's magazine who I always suspected was queer himself—that kept me on the payroll, but it was barely enough to cover rent, food, and transit.

Now that my income could no longer sustain all the drinking and partying, many of my night companions slowly faded away. Some shunned me altogether, fearing the infection of outness. I no longer received invites to parties, and a number of friends stopped picking up the phone when I called. My lights at home dimmed before eleven in the evening as I watched reruns of sitcoms on television until I passed out on the sofa, covered in fast-food crumbs.

One evening I got a frantic phone call from the green-eyed bald man, whom I'd continued to occasionally meet up with. "You're out of the closet now?"

"Not by choice I'm not," I said.

"What does that even mean?" He sounded terrified, as if he were talking to an actual boogeyman who'd escaped a childhood closet.

"I'm not sure anymore."

"Don't call me again." He hung up.

MOTHER(S)

R U dead?

After a year and a half of radio silence, Shiraz messaged me out of the blue on Facebook Chat.

Very much a ghost by now, I replied.

I need a favour. Can you come downtown?

I stared at the message. I hadn't been in downtown Cairo for over a year, rarely venturing outside the home I shared with a boyfriend on the outskirts of Giza. With our view of the pyramids, our L-shaped sectional, and our two dogs who took turns sleeping in my lap, why would I ever leave?

Kamal and I had been dating for a bit over a year. "Dating" here implies that we actually went on dates, which isn't true. Our courtship played out away from public scrutiny, in his three-bedroom penthouse apartment. Within the walls of his home Kamal was safe to be the queer man he wanted to be, free of the consequences society burdened us with.

After my experience in Cairo, I too wanted to disappear.

Most nights we hung out in Kamal's living room and watched movies or concert DVDs from his massive collection. He had a lady who cleaned the house and cooked for both him and his dogs, who were on a specific diet. He also had a driver who did his shopping and paid his bills. His mother, a French woman who'd married his Egyptian father back in the seventies, bought his clothes for him.

Kamal used to be a dancer. After falling out with the head of his company he'd started his own studio, teaching aerobics, step, tango, cha-cha, and salsa. Later he added yoga to his practice, much to my dismay—he wouldn't shut up about it.

Three weeks into dating, Kamal invited me to move in with him, and I said yes. Weeks later, I knew I'd made a mistake. Kamal was controlling and overbearing, and we had very little in common. However, I decided to stay, knowing well that I had very few other options.

Does that make me an opportunist? I felt love for Kamal. Maybe not a Disney movie love, but some form of it. Mostly I was attracted to the life he had, mesmerized by its safety.

"He came to me crying back when he was your age," his mother had told me over dinner while his father sat silently across the table. "He said that other students at his university were bullying him, calling him names."

That night she'd asked Kamal if he was gay, and he took his time to answer.

"That's when I knew that what I'd suspected for years was true." Kamal's mother passed the salt to her son. "He didn't have to say a word. A mother's heart knows." She took him out of school and paid for private classes to finish his dance practice.

Kamal and I wouldn't last the year. We would break up in a month or two. One too many fights revealed what we both knew deep down inside: that we weren't meant for each other. It was a relationship of convenience—I needed an escape from Cairo, and he needed an *insert-here* boyfriend to share the splendour of his home. There was a sense of security in my isolation. I had swung between Ahmad and Danny for far too long, and now I just wanted to stand still and breathe. *We'll break up one day soon,* I told myself. *But for now, this works. This feels safe.* That's the thing about living as a queer person in a homophobic community: you learn to survive it whichever way you can.

Kamal taught me how to dance, then taught me how to teach others how to dance. I neglected my writing and instead focused my energy on becoming a fitness instructor in his studio. I amassed a small following teaching private classes, and soon I was in the best shape of my life. Feeling handsome, slender, and desirable, I marvelled at my naked body in the mirror: the way my chest curved, my abs popped, and my calves rounded like half-moons. I straightened my hair, dyed it a midday blue, and wore crop tops that showcased my waistline. I trimmed my body hair painfully short but kept the stubble on my face.

Hey, are you still there? Can you come? Shiraz wrote.

What do you need? I pressed.

I need you to go somewhere with me. I'll explain everything when I see you.

●

A couple of days later Shiraz and I sat in the backseat of Kamal's car. We avoided the questions in the driver's eyes, who asked twice if we really wanted to go to Shubra.

"It's no place for people like you."

The driver climbed a bridge ramp, then picked up speed as he crossed the Nile into downtown, leaving the rest of the city behind us and avoiding Zamalek Island with its old-money homes and massive luxury hotels. We turned onto a stretch of road where high white walls obstructed our view of the surrounding neighbourhoods, leaving us with only the sky to look up at. As on most days in Cairo, it was clear and blue and endless. No wonder the ancient Egyptians worshipped its sun.

"Did you know they built these walls to hide the slums from the eyes of tourists driving to the pyramids?" I said. Shiraz flashed me a dirty look. I kept my mouth shut until we reached the off-ramp to Shubra and the driver let us out at the corner Shiraz had pointed to.

"Just be careful here, Danny," the driver instructed. "Try to be less—"

"Obvious?" I said.

"Yes. Obvious."

We got out and were met by the heat of the day. Shiraz pulled a piece of paper from her pocket, studied it, and then we set off.

Shubra welcomed us with its busy streets, its buildings painted cheaply in faded yellows and murky browns, crispy under the harsh sunlight. People walked in all directions, sweat under their arms and down their backs; stray dogs hid in the shade behind piles of garbage and a stale-meat smell emanated from restaurants and shops.

"Watch out!" someone shouted from behind me. I jumped out of the way of a delivery boy balancing loaves of fresh bread on a board over his head, steering his bicycle with one hand as he steadied his precious cargo with the other.

The men around us were threadlike thin and hurried about in cheap designer knockoff T-shirts. The women, all in black and brown niqabs hiding most of their features, walked more slowly and in groups of twos and threes. They took their time, examining everyone around them like a herd of ptarmigans fearing a predator.

It grew quieter and calmer the deeper we went into the neighbourhood. Eventually the sidewalks disappeared and we walked on the narrow streets, leaving enough room for a stray car to pass by. The heat intensified. As people watched us pass from their windows, we ignored their whispers and questions.

"Are you okay?" I asked Shiraz. "Do you need to take a moment?" I was the one who needed a moment.

"Let's keep walking," she said. Finally we reached the building marked on her piece of paper. We descended the stairs to the smell of mould and a gate with no doorbell.

A woman in a hijab creaked the door ajar and examined us, her suspicious gaze lingering on my blue hair that she could see peeking out from under the cap I wore for the occasion. Then she opened the door wider and nodded at us to enter.

"Are you the father?" she asked.

"He's just a friend," Shiraz said.

"Friendships with men always bring girls like you to my house," the woman said, tightening the hijab over her head. We arrived at a windowless room and sat on the sofa. The only noise was the hushed reading of the Quran from a mounted TV. "How far along are you?"

"I missed my period last month," Shiraz said.

The two discussed the money, which had been agreed upon over the phone, then Shiraz handed over a large sum of cash from the belt tightly wrapped around her waist. The woman licked her thumb and pointer and counted the bills, mumbling the numbers to herself.

"The procedure takes at least an hour," she said. "Your friend can wait here while we go to the bedroom. I have some numbing medication that I will inject you with, but it will probably be painful."

"You're not going to try to talk me out of it?" Shiraz asked.

"Girl," the woman said, "if you found me, you've already made up your mind."

She left the room and kept the door behind her half closed. We sat in silence for a moment, then Shiraz stood up.

"Do you want me to talk you out of it?" I asked.

"What options do I have, Danny?"

Shiraz had fallen in love with a sweet man from Alexandria who came from a conservative Coptic Christian family. A teacher at an elementary school, loved both by his students and their parents, he was soft-spoken and well-educated, and he loved her back. As a woman born to a Muslim family, though, it was illegal for Shiraz to marry a non-Muslim.

She'd meet her lover in the room he rented whenever he visited Cairo. Her friends would cover for her when she spent afternoons with him, telling her family she was at the library or at her part-time job. The line of men asking for her hand in marriage lingered for a while, then the numbers dwindled as she continued to reject their proposals. As a woman in her mid-twenties, she now had to accept her fate and marry a man her family insisted on. And so she'd broken it off with the Alexandrian, only to find out a week or so later that she was pregnant.

Shiraz disappeared behind the opened door. Moments later a steady hand slammed it shut and I was left alone in the living room, surrounded by walls without windows. A sense of claustrophobia pressed in on me. I stood up and paced the floor. The Quran reading that played on the TV seemed to get louder and sharper. The reader's voice rose higher in tone as he put stress on the *khaas*, hiccupped his *dhaas*, and rolled his *raas*.

I thought I heard a moan of pain but couldn't tell. I searched around for a remote control to mute the Quran reader but couldn't find one. Finally I stood on the sofa under the TV and manually turned it off, drowning the room in silence. I couldn't place the lost moan again.

My phone lit up with a message from Kamal, but I ignored it. Instead I opened my contact list and scrolled to the number for my grandparents' apartment in Damascus, where my mother lived.

No one in Egypt knew much about my family. In my back story, lazily crafted and full of holes, my mother was dead. I kept her number in my phone like a dirty secret, unable to let it go. In my head she remained frozen in time, never changing or growing older. She occupied the same world and repeated the same delusions, accusing neighbours of witchcraft and cursing the ghosts in the walls. Still, in that moment, I wanted to hear her voice. I wanted to know that she was all right.

That was the day a nagging idea took root: my mother's life could have been much better if I'd been aborted. As soon as it popped into my mind I wanted to crumble it between my fingers, swallow it, disappear it forever. Instead it got bigger and bigger until it was all I could think about.

The thought persisted for so long that six months later I finally got on an airplane and flew to Damascus to see my mother.

I was on the steps of a restaurant when she showed up, flanked by my sisters. Nour, now seventeen and about to leave for college, wore her newfound hijab so tightly it made her oval face appear even rounder. Lara was quiet, appearing to judge silently with her eyes.

"Come down and say hello to your mother," Nour said. My mother looked up at me. She didn't comment on my hair, dark roots now growing in beneath the frosty blue tips. Her face looked scratched, then powdered over with layers of foundation. The pink gloss on her lips, perhaps intended to make her look younger, had the opposite effect. Her clothes were dishevelled and wrinkled, as if she'd rushed out the door last-minute.

My mother frightened me. I was not twenty-four anymore. I was a child of ten again.

"Come down," Nour insisted. "Why are you standing there like an idiot?"

I took a few hesitant steps toward them and extended a hand. My mother gave me hers, which I printed with a kiss and pressed to my forehead, a sign of respect. But when she opened her arms for a hug I jumped back like a scared kitten. My sisters laughed the awkwardness away.

They'd been seeing her once every two weeks for the past five years. Since the divorce, the family law court in Damascus had given my mother supervised visitation rights, which a couple of years later were loosened to unsupervised visits. Nour told me that the encounters were almost funny in how identical they were. My mother appeared in the same outfit, asked the same questions, and didn't seem to listen to any of the answers. She insisted on meeting at the same restaurant and ordered the one meal for everyone.

"She lost her shit once," Nour whispered. "She told us that a famous Lebanese singer was in love with her and that we must all run away from Syria together so that she can marry him."

My mother and I sat across the table from each other. The restaurant staff knew her and snuck glances at us while rolling sandwiches and decorating dishes with pickles and spices.

"How are you all? How are your lives? What are you eating, what are you drinking? How are your children?" my mother asked, seemingly on autopilot.

"Mama, I'm twenty-four, I don't have children."

I did the math in my head: when she was my age, I was seven. No wonder she kept asking about our children. For a moment, sadness took over. What life did this woman have to give up to become a conduit for someone else's? I reached for her hand, but she snapped it away as if I were a snake.

"Don't touch me, your hands are too cold." Her voice got louder.

"Mom, I just held your hand outside," I whispered. Restaurant staff had begun to peer at us, so I put on a fake smile. "It's okay. I won't touch you."

"Why are your hands cold?"

"I just washed them with cold water," I lied.

"No. Your hands are too cold. What are you?" My sisters cowered in their seats. This was not the first time they'd witnessed a display like this. The restaurant staff monitored us like hawks. "What do you want from me? Why won't you leave me alone?"

My shoulders tightened. I fought the urge to run out of the restaurant, the neighbourhood, the city, the country.

"Mama, calm down," Nour said. "It's all going to be okay, I promise you."

My mother looked around nervously, as if she were surrounded by shadows. She took a deep breath, then rested both hands flat on the table and whispered to herself. The restaurant owner stood watching for a bit, then took a couple of steps back and busied himself behind the cashier. From that point on, I stayed silent. My breathing was shallow but my heartbeat was loud. *I shouldn't have come*, I thought. The next hour was a blur, and then she was gone.

That was the last time I ever saw my mother. Her mental health continued to deteriorate over the years, and our paths diverged further the deeper she submerged into those dark waters. In the last voicemail she left me before her death, twenty years after the broken window incident I'd witnessed in my teens, my mother repeats what she'd said that day: "I am cursed. I was cursed by witches years ago. They made your father hate me. They took away our home." A silence follows, then she switches gears, as if she's caught sight of her own illusion. "How are you? How are your children? How is the weather? How is your life?" She sounds like a computer-generated mother. "Tell me what you do and when you do it. Tell me about your days." Her voice is high-pitched yet monotonous, lacking in colour—a harboured ship creaking with the waves, but not a soul on board. "What do you eat? What do you drink?"

I saved the voicemail, motivated by what can only be described as penance, but I never replied. I hadn't responded to any of my mother's messages, which by then had come about once a year for the past decade. She repeated her conspiracies about ghosts and witches, spoke to me as if she'd forgotten my name, and asked about children who'd never existed.

A couple of days after it arrived, my sister informed me that my mother had passed away from Covid-related complications. In the two weeks that followed I played her final voicemail dozens of times, searching for traces of my mother in the flat foreign voice.

I never found her.

·

The door to the backroom opened and Shiraz walked out, jaundiced and unsteady. I stood up and she leaned on me until she reached the sofa, where she sat with difficulty.

The woman followed behind her, her hands smelling of fresh soap. She handed me some medication and told me to make sure Shiraz got two pills every eight hours. Shiraz snatched them out of my hand, lifted her T-shirt, and stuffed them into her waist belt.

"I can sew back your hymen for your wedding night," the woman said. "You'll have to come back in a couple weeks, and it will cost you extra."

Shiraz said nothing. She placed a hand on my shoulder and lifted herself up.

"You have to rest here for an hour or two before you leave," the woman instructed, but Shiraz shook her head.

"Let's just wait an hour," I said.

"No. I want to leave now."

The woman shrugged and stepped out of the way as I helped Shiraz to the door.

Outside, we retraced our steps back to the main road, Shiraz leaning on me like a cane. We'd stop every once in a while and she'd press her lower abdomen.

Eventually we reached the car and shuffled into the backseat. The driver looked at us in the rear-view mirror, checking on Shiraz and locking eyes with me. Later, when we dropped Shiraz near her home, I asked the driver to follow her slowly until she reached her building.

Finally we got on the highway. The traffic lightened and the roads got wider as we left behind the buildings crowding the city, their residents peering out at us. Now the villas on the outskirts of Cairo saluted us with their high hedges and glimmering windows. Fancy cars replaced the aging public transport buses. I put my sunglasses on, removed my cap, rested my head back, and asked the driver to turn on the AC. The echoes of thoughts I would rather forget filled my head; I breathed them out in deep sighs. Soon Kamal's building appeared from afar: tall, majestic, and topped with its inviting penthouse. I took off the light shirt I had on, revealing the skimpy tank top I wore beneath. I waved goodbye to the driver. Then, in the building's gate, I saw myself in the darkened glass. I looked nothing like the boy who'd grown up in Syria. The thing is—I liked it.

REVOLUTION

It started with whispers.

By 2010 the unrest in Egyptian streets was growing. There was a farmers' sit-in outside the Ministry of Agriculture denouncing the astronomical increase in taxes. A line of workers, with small signs and tired faces, crowded the sidewalk next to the Parliament demanding fair pay for hard work. Photos and videos of the Tunisian man who'd set himself on fire to protest poverty and police brutality were shared, re-shared, and analyzed on Egyptian talk shows and private Facebook profiles. Like the whistling of a pressure cooker, it went unnoticed at first. Then slowly it got louder until it filled the whole city with sirens.

A story that had been asleep for months reawakened. Khaled Saeed, a young man who'd died in police custody in the coastal city of Alexandria, became a rallying point for many of the anti-regime activists on the ground. A Facebook group called We Are All Khaled Saeed became the operation room for many of the protests, which began online and gained steady momentum.

Overnight, a sad-looking wall in downtown Cairo was graced with a mural of two policemen holding a mother captive by the shoulders. People caught it in the corner of their eye on their way to work, too afraid to pause and take it in. By evening policemen had painted over it with a fresh coat of white. Slogans like *We Are All Khaled* and *Bread, Freedom, and Social Justice* appeared on the walls of subway cars and metro stations. Someone was caught attempting to spray-paint signs for Hosni Mubarak Station red.

Misinformation circulated online: posts by strangers, shared by friends, claimed that someone in such-and-such Egyptian town had also set himself on fire. Other posts corrected the unconfirmed reports, claiming it was a different town. Some posts asserted that the man was mentally unwell. In some stories the man survived, in others he died a painful death, and in yet others he turned up elsewhere claiming he'd never set himself ablaze in the first place.

Then came the Facebook events: secret at first to protect the identities of the organizers, then eventually shared publicly without fear. The invitations directed people to light candles in their windows on a certain Friday to show support for the Tunisian revolution next door. We were asked to wear white T-shirts the following Friday and walk the streets at a specific hour. Finally, in January of 2011, came a Facebook event invite that was accepted by millions, calling for a protest in the streets that would gather at Tahrir Square in central Cairo.

They called it the Friday of Anger.

After my inevitable breakup with Kamal, I had returned to the heart of Cairo.

I hoped enough time had passed that people would have forgotten all about Ahmad Ramadan and his homosexual ways. They hadn't. The city remembered my sins; my job applications were again rejected. So I relied on the gig economy, continuing freelance work at the Saudi children's magazine and teaching aerobics at a couple of fitness centres. Meanwhile I rented a small room in a shared apartment with two foreigners who studied at the American University in Cairo.

And I made friends with Western expats living in Cairo. We travelled around Egypt together; I proved useful as their unofficial translator. I received invites to their house parties, hosted in massive rentals on the island of Zamalek or in the central neighbourhood of Garden City. Then I began to date exclusively within their pool: an Italian with the most beautiful hazel eyes I'd ever seen; an American with nerdy glasses and shaggy blond hair.

When people asked my name, I said Danny. I'd given up attempting to balance the two personas and decided to merge them into one: a queer man who happened to be an author. Everyone who knew me knew I was gay, from the rich Egyptian clients in my fitness classes to the foreigners at their house parties.

Does that sound brave? Let me explain: I'd become an expert at sniffing out homophobia. I befriended only those who I knew would be accepting, and I refused to be friends with anyone I'd have to lie to about my sexuality. I curated my own social experience, carving out a community of mostly young white folks and other queer brown men.

I returned to writing, feverishly producing enough short stories to fill a whole second collection within six months. They featured characters navigating love/hate relationships, fantastical creatures thrown into mundane realistic situations, and imaginative storytellers forced to face their dwindling memories.

Through my new friends I eventually landed a steady job at an English-language newspaper that employed a mix of young liberal Egyptians and foreign journalists. The interview was short. I'd met the office manager at a house party; we were friendly, and he knew of my queerness. I had finally found a slice of Cairo where I could be professionally out of the closet.

If things had stayed the way they were, I'd probably still be in that part of the world, doing that type of work. I was, dare I say, finally content with where my life was going. My fellow journalists liked me, and the work was meaningful. I interviewed international celebrities coming to the Cairo Film Festival and hired other queer writers to review the latest novels. I received recognition for my good management skills.

Two days before the Friday of Anger the newspaper sent out an organization-wide email calling a mandatory meeting at a godawful early hour. I wasn't usually invited to such gatherings, which tended to be for the political journalists, mostly white foreigners with sticker-covered laptops and unironic Palestinian keffiyehs tightly knotted around their necks. These folks were used to owning the meeting room for hours, loudly discussing the politics of the day and leaving half-eaten pastries for the rest of us.

Everyone trickled into the office, a dusty old building in one of Cairo's historic neighbourhoods. We made quick Turkish coffees or snatched a free water bottle from the mini-fridge next to the accountant's office. My colleagues filed into the boardroom: the woman who ran the health and fitness page, tan lines visible from her latest trip to the Red Sea; the twentysomething muscle bro from Arizona looking to break the story that would secure him a job at *The New York Times*; the copy editor, a middle-aged British woman who gently corrected my English and offered positive editorial notes on my columns; a young Egyptian political journalist who dressed exclusively in traditional jilbabs. Then there was me: the queer kid with the dyed red hair who wrote a series about his love for different streets in Cairo and reviewed the latest *Mission: Impossible* movie.

In walked the chief editor. I'd be lying if I said I had a lot of love for her; I believe she viewed my role as a necessary evil, a survival tactic to ensure that the newspaper wouldn't be viewed as an absolute leftist anti-government pamphlet. She'd treated me coldly ever since my first day and seemed to have eyes only for the white journalists, who gathered in her office to smoke cigarettes, drink beer, and discuss the day's happenings. I rarely found value in her writing, which was inaccessible to the everyday, non-fluent English speaker in a way that felt deliberate.

She scanned the room. "The new world is about to be born," she said with gravitas, as if performing on a stage, "and we will be its witnesses."

People around the room nodded. I struggled to not roll my eyes.

"For the next two days we will scatter the streets. Search for stories. Take photos. Record videos. But always do so in groups—no one should be alone. Especially you." She nodded at the foreigners.

"Is there a possibility we could be arrested?" the copy editor asked.

"Yes. This will be our last meeting in the office. Police raids are a real possibility now, and we can't be gathered here like sitting ducks."

I recoiled. I was on an ever-renewable tourist visa in Egypt. If I was arrested, I'd be deported to Syria. I'm not sure why I so feared the return to my home country. Perhaps the thought of going back felt too vivid a symbol of my failure to make a life for myself here.

"How long do you expect this to last?" I asked.

The chief editor seemed to register that I'd spoken out of turn. "I think it will be a few days until he steps down," she said, referring to the president. Tunisia's dictator had been forced out mere days before. "Be careful out there, and take in this historic moment. We are lucky to be alive today."

The political journalists divided up, each group including a local who spoke Arabic. I stood waiting and was eventually approached by Mia, an American journalist I'd worked with a couple times.

"Do you want to walk with me? You can translate, and we can explore the city together."

I nodded, and she ran to her office to grab her camera.

Mia had had one or two stories go viral. She had a local boyfriend, a handsome Egyptian man she paraded around at house parties for her fellow foreigners. When she found out the year before that I was gay she'd gasped with wide eyes, touched my forearm gently, and repeatedly told me how brave I was.

The Egyptian who wore jilbabs told me to be careful. "White journalists come from the other side of the world, work people of colour like us to the bone researching and translating and building their stories, then put their names in the bylines and drop us to a quick mention at the bottom of the article."

It was the first time I'd heard the term "people of colour." I was baffled.

"Ready to go?" Mia emerged, her huge Canon camera strapped around her neck.

When Mia and I left the building, the city was still maintaining its eerie morning silence.

"Maybe the major roads are as busy as usual?" She led us toward Qasr El Eyni Street. As we approached, it became clear: the main road was just as quiet as the back alleyways.

"Look." Mia pointed to a hastily built police checkpoint at the top of the street. Two large, armed police vehicles blocked the road, about a dozen officers standing around it on guard.

"Don't point," I said. "They don't want people to easily reach Tahrir Square. Clearly they're prepared for possible protests on Friday."

Mia was a year younger than me and had come to Egypt to study at the American University in Cairo. After landing a job at the newspaper, she refocused her career on political writing. She walked the streets of Cairo with the air of Rachel Weisz's character in *The Mummy*: a blend of fascination and self-assurance, as if she knew all there was to know about Egyptian politics but kept it to herself so as not to offend the locals.

"Hold my hand," she said. "Let's walk as if we're taking a stroll."

"I don't think that's a good idea," I said. "We'll attract more attention that way. Egyptians don't take kindly to a man and a woman holding hands."

"Right, right."

"Here." I removed my backpack and offered it to her. "Put your camera inside this. I can carry it for you."

We walked toward Tahrir Square, named after the Arabic word for freedom. Surrounding it was the French quarter, with its glamorous late nineteenth-century buildings that had seen better days; the Egyptian Museum, with its precious historic treasures; the bridge, flanked by two lion statues, crossing the Nile to the rich neighbourhoods of Mohandiseen and Zamalek; and the Mogamma, the government headquarters in an office building as large as a mountain. The square was the city's beating heart and the streets its arteries, bringing visitors in and pumping them back out. It was dense with shops and shisha cafés, with barely an empty inch of asphalt in sight, but today the vendors were closed all the way down Qasr El Eyni. When we arrived we saw that it was filled with officers clad identically in brown. Mia and I stood in the distance, watching them create barriers at every possible entry to and exit from the square: a human fence at every sidewalk. Officers reached their assigned posts and froze in place, eyes following their commanders, mostly older men with large bellies and salt-and-pepper moustaches.

"It's a show of force," Mia whispered.

She walked toward the square; after a moment of hesitation I followed her. We arrived at a wall of soldiers, and before I could say anything Mia spoke to them in her broken Arabic. They didn't even acknowledge her.

"Hey, it's okay. Can I handle this? Let me handle this." I asked them how to cross the road into Tahrir. "We want to cross, sir." I pointed to the university buildings, surrounded by more officers.

"Why?" asked the commander at the helm of the human fence.

"She lives in the Greek Campus at AUC," I said, gesturing to Mia. "I'm just walking her home."

The commander, who clearly hadn't had a good night's sleep, ping-ponged his gaze between the two of us. Beyond the row of soldiers we could make out a gathering of policemen, cursing and circling something on the ground.

"Is she your girlfriend?" he asked, ignoring the debacle behind him.

"Yes."

"How long have you been together?" There was movement among the circle of policemen, my view of its cause obstructed by other officers lining the sidewalk. They jumped, cursed, knelt, stood up.

"A couple of months, sir." Mia attempted to grab my hand, but I quickly snapped it out of reach.

He tilted his head, looked Mia up and down, then returned his gaze to me.

"Do you know how to fuck her well?"

I heard a chuckle from the line of soldiers. Mia gasped. I followed her gaze across the street, where two of the circling policemen were lifting the body of a young boy off the concrete. They had clearly kicked him while he was down; his face was bloodied and his clothes were torn. He didn't resist or scream as they dragged him into a leather shop. The rest of the soldiers quickly found their spots in the human fence.

"I—I think we'll walk another way," I told the officer, who smirked. He ushered the soldiers around him to open up and invited us to cross.

"It's okay. You can go."

Mia and I exchanged looks, then stepped into the empty road. On the ground we could see the trail of blood leading to the leather shop, guarded now by the two policemen.

"Can I take a photo of this?" Mia whispered.

"Shush."

We continued down the road, quickening our step, leaving Tahrir Square behind. With the winter sun intensifying as we reached the Nile Hilton hotel, I took off my leather jacket and hugged it between my arms. Mia stood dazed, then reached for my backpack and pulled out her camera. "We should have taken photos, Danny."

"We would have been arrested."

"So what?" She placed the camera up against her face and dialed its lens to zoom in on the officers.

"I don't have a fucking embassy to get me out of an Egyptian jail, lady."

She lowered her camera, put a hand on my shoulder, and smiled as if to assure me. "I will make sure the American embassy gets us both out if we're arrested."

"You're delusional. I can't even walk the streets around the American embassy."

"You sound very angry," she said. "I need you to calm down." I took a deep breath and marched away, and Mia followed. We turned onto a side street lined with old theatres and hand-painted movie posters.

"Danny, you don't understand. This is the story of a lifetime. This is the moment history is made. I need to be part of this."

"Why?" I said with a calmer voice. "So you can record it?"

"Yes. For everyone to see back home."

"Why does that matter?"

"It's the work of the journalist."

"Yes, but what about the boy?"

"What boy?"

"The one we saw beaten up. Is he part of the revolution? What's his story?"

Mia stopped walking. "We should go back," she said. "You have a BlackBerry. You can use it to record a short video of where the arrest happened. I'll tweet the video after."

I stood in silence, looking at her.

"It's a good story, Danny."

From behind us, on the road under the October Bridge, the chants came. We turned around and saw our first protest. Young Egyptian men and women filled the streets shouting the slogans we'd seen online.

By the time we reached the main road, the protest had taken a turn toward Tahrir Square, and we followed it. The human fence quickly scattered when faced with the large number of protesters.

"We should go in deeper," Mia said.

"Mia, hold on. Slow down." She was giddy as a child on Christmas morning and acting as if she were invincible. She raised her camera over her head and clicked the shutter repeatedly, taking blind photos in every direction. A group of protesters gathered around a parked police car. They lined one side of it, slipped their palms under its metal, and then, with one swift shout, they flipped it upside down. Teenagers screamed in joy. Horns echoed from every corner.

Windows opened, and people chanted. Heads peered down from atop the bridge. One man, shirtless, climbed up a traffic light for a better view of the square.

What the fuck. What the fuck. What the fuck, I repeated under my breath. There was a lot happening all at once. I knew I had to stay with Mia, but otherwise my brain was filled with half-finished sentences.

"Mia! Stay with me!" I shouted. She was being swallowed by the crowd, although I could still see the camera held over her head. When she finally turned around, panic rippled across her face. I grabbed her and dragged her to the side of the street away from the protest. We returned to the entrance of the Nile Hilton and stood at the corner.

"You okay?"

She nodded. Her pupils were narrow and focused, and the soft hairs on her wrists stood up. She reviewed the last few photos she'd taken.

Then we heard the drumming.

From our vantage point we could see a line of armed police officers approaching with anti-riot gear and masks on their faces. They used batons to rhythmically knock their shields as they forced the protesters into the road leading to Tahrir Square. Within seconds the protesters were blocked—encircled now by the human fence, the riot police behind them. Two of the latter pointed their guns to the sky; loud shots rang out before cans leaking tear gas landed in the crowd.

"Fuck!" I shouted. The riot police headed our way.

The protesters, realizing they were trapped, panicked. The flow of the group changed: instead of the focused flood moving toward the square, they scattered in every direction. But the human fence moved, forcing them to a tighter spot. The riot police got closer to us. We were kettled in.

"We need to get out of here." Mia's panic filled the air between us. "We'll be trampled under this crowd."

People rushed by us with bottles of soda that they poured into the eyes of those affected by tear gas. The flipped police car caught on fire. Flames grew within it quickly; it looked like a funeral pyre. I pulled my phone out, took a photo, and uploaded it to Facebook.

"What are you doing?" Mia asked.

"I don't know."

"Psst."

We turned around to see a hotel security guard holding a side door open for us. We ran through, followed by five or six others, before the guard shut the door and locked it.

"There's an elevator at the end of this hallway," he said. "Go to the sixteenth floor. The wedding hall is empty. Hide there, and I'll come get you."

Mia, still holding her camera tight between her palms, followed me as we ran toward the elevator. Soon we found ourselves in the wedding hall, its floor-to-ceiling windows overlooking Tahrir Square.

In the cold room, I realized I'd lost my jacket. I hugged my upper body and shivered.

"Wow," Mia said quietly. She got up close to the windows and took photos. We stood there for hours looking at Tahrir Square fogged with tear gas. More protesters joined. Then more. Then more. Then more.

In early February of 2011, at eleven in the morning, I left Egypt.

In the week following my night on the floor of the Hilton's wedding hall, I'd gained an immense amount of information on dictatorships, propaganda media, and the local, regional, and international influences in the Middle East and North African region. I basically received a crash course in local politics from a group of angry activists and motivated journalists.

All able and willing reporters at the newspaper had moved into a hotel together since the morning of the Friday of Anger. The Egyptian regime had entirely closed down phone, data, and internet service, but when we discovered that a couple of hotels still had access to the web through satellite, we quickly pooled our resources and rented a room in one with a balcony overlooking the Qasr El Nil Bridge. We watched in horror as the regime used water cannons and tear gas on the protesters to deny them access to downtown.

"Let us through, let us through!" the protesters repeated. They jumped up and down in unison, the bridge shaking under their feet.

We took photos and posted them on the paper's website and on our Facebook and Twitter accounts. For days we were among a very small contingent of voices coming out of a darkened Egypt.

I fell asleep on the hotel room floor amid conversations about why the world around me was changing. I woke up to the same conversations with my morning instant coffee.

Many of my tweets went viral, and I was quickly verified on Twitter. Soon I was writing articles for international newspapers—covering the situation on the ground, the security around the Egyptian

Museum, the graffiti defacing military tanks, and the moment the regime finally gave up on Tahrir Square, ceding it to the protesters.

As journalists from all over the world gathered in Cairo, a herd of widely recognized names appeared among the protests. They wore yellow vests, brought their own camera crews, and held microphones marked with international news agency logos. The square buzzed with spotlights.

On Tuesday, the first of February, I was assigned to go with Mia to the neighbourhood of Giza, a pro-regime section of the city, to investigate why some Egyptians still supported Hosni Mubarak's government.

What started as a quick morning assignment exceeded our expectations. Within moments of our arrival, and before we could ask any questions, a man pointed at Mia and her camera. "These are the agents of the foreign media," he shouted. "They want to destroy our country!"

"No, we're on your side," I said.

"He's a criminal. Look at his tattoos! They're prison tattoos!"

Suddenly a crowd had gathered around us. Mia burrowed into my side. When someone pulled on her camera, she screamed and hugged it closer to her chest.

"Leave it alone!" she shouted. "Leave us alone."

I drew Mia in closer and asserted that we weren't criminals, but no one heard me. All I could see were the angry faces swarming us. A tall, broad-shouldered Egyptian man stepped forward, raised his hands, and commanded everyone to listen, but he was ignored. He asked me a question that was swallowed up by the noise around us.

"I can't hear you," I said.

Then I felt someone's arms around me, grabbing me by the waist and pulling me back, a reverse bear hug. I clung to Mia and screamed. I heard her scream, too. Someone snapped the camera off her chest and a woman grabbed her by the hair.

I tried to free myself from the arms of the person behind me and was smacked on the back of the head, then again, then a third time. My ears rang and my vision blurred. Mia's voice came from within a deep well.

"Stop it! Stop it!" she shouted.

Suddenly, as quickly as it had begun, the melee was broken up by a pair of policemen. I was dizzy, as if I'd spun around in circles for an hour. I couldn't keep my head up straight.

"What's happening here?" an officer asked, and a chorus of voices attempted to answer at once.

"I'm not feeling well," I told Mia. She looked at me with panic in her eyes, pulled a napkin out of her pocket, and dried the side of my face and around my ears. When she withdrew her hand I saw red on the napkin.

"I'm not bleeding," I said, but I felt as if I was about to vomit.

The officers talked to the crowd. Mia showed her American passport, and soon we were being driven away in a police car.

"Where are we going?" I asked.

"Try to rest," she said. "We're going to a hospital."

I leaned back and closed my eyes.

When I came to, it was nighttime. I was back in the hotel room, on a bed with three colleagues from the newspaper. Mia explained that none of the hospitals she tried would admit me. She thought I might have a concussion. Apparently I'd made no sense for the past couple of hours. "How are you feeling?"

"Not too bad," I said. "I'm sorry you lost your camera."

She pulled the camera off the bedside table, a look of victory in her eyes, and told me that the policemen had managed to get it back. She'd paid them to release us and hand over the equipment.

"See? I told you I'd take care of you."

The next day I woke up feeling better. After breakfast, I told everyone I was ready to go back out into the streets.

"Maybe take the day off," the chief editor said. She'd begun to soften toward me. After assuring everyone that I'd be fine, Mia and I stepped out into the street to join the protesters. It didn't take long for me to realize I wasn't fine. As I stood on the corner of Tahrir Square, press badge in hand, I froze. Everything around me seemed to unfold in slow motion: every twitch on every face, the click of a lighter lighting up a smoke, the crackle of electricity in a megaphone held up high. I felt the heat of the sun on my forehead and the breeze of the Nile on my back. I was both warm and cold at the same time. In my mouth, I tasted blood.

"Danny, are you okay?" Mia asked.

"Let's go back inside."

"We just left."

"I need to go back inside."

That evening, Mia texted an ex-boyfriend of mine—an Italian man who'd spent more time hating me for breaking up with him than he had loving me when we were together. He was being evacuated to Jordan by the NGO he worked for. "You're still my plus-one in our evacuation plan, if you want to take the spot," he said. I did.

The next day I called Shiraz from my taxi to the airport to see if she was okay. Her biggest concern was her parents, who insisted that criminals who'd escaped prisons around Cairo would come to murder them all in their sleep. She asked if I was leaving for good.

"Just a couple of weeks and I'll be back."

"Okay. I'll see you in a couple of weeks," she said.

I left Egypt on an airplane to Jordan, then said my goodbyes to the Italian and took a taxi to Damascus. The next time I'd visit Cairo would be eleven years later, returning as a Canadian man.

PILLARS

"In February 2011, I went back to Syria seeking the sense of belonging that I so wanted," I said, pacing the green room. "Seeking the sense of belonging," I repeated, "seeking the sense of belonging."

"You nervous?" a fellow speaker asked.

"I am now," I joked. We both laughed.

I'd prepared for this TEDx talk for weeks, but the lines refused to stay in my mind. Finally, the organizers allowed me to bring cue cards onstage. I clutched my notes like a safety blanket.

"You're the final speaker," the guy said. "It's an honour."

"Or a burden. It means I'll be nervous all day."

In an earlier draft of the speech, which I'd practised with the event organizers, I went into more detail about my goodbye to Egypt: the hugs, the promises to return, the longing for friends I lost, the Syrian passport I couldn't renew. The unrealistic fear that I'd burned all my bridges in Cairo. The organizers nodded, the public speaking specialist took notes, and someone ran a timer. My speech went well over the allotted eighteen minutes.

"Well, about Egypt," the specialist said. "Maybe try to simplify it to focus the story. That would be better, right?"

Audiences prefer a simple and digestible narrative, he explained, reminding me that I'd been selected to give a speech about the Syrian refugee experience. "Think about your listeners," he added. "The narrative needs to be smooth. Maybe skip over Egypt and jump directly back to Syria."

"I didn't just jump into Syria from Egypt, though."

"Yes. Of course," he said, "but the audience doesn't need to know that. Let's edit out the Egypt stories for time. Just say something about going back to Syria seeking a sense of belonging or some such thing."

I nodded.

When the time came, I was welcomed onto the stage with roaring applause. My fingers left sweaty prints on the cue cards, now curved by the pressure of my grip. I took a loud breath in, caught on the mic, and held it in my chest. "I want you," I began, my voice hoarse, not yet ready, "I want you to imagine yourself as a tree.

"A beautiful, evergreen, fully grown tree that carries fruits and delicious berries." My neck was stiff, my chest tight. The tree metaphor grew as I shifted the focus to Syria, "a place where there's a war on trees. There are those who want to cut down all trees, to burn them to ashes."

I snickered nervously throughout the first few minutes, but then my smile turned genuine. When I joked about my trauma, the audience felt permitted to laugh. Drenched in darkness, evident only through their chuckles, they felt less hostile. My storytelling became authentic.

"But I believe that every tree has a role to play in the ecosystem that it's part of." I reached the core of my speech, what I was meant to tell. "I believe that my role was to support the LGBTQ community in Syria."

In the raw video I received of the TEDx talk weeks later, the two audience members sitting right below the camera were caught conversing after my speech had ended.

"This was very good," one said.

"He knows how to tell a good story," said the other.

◖

Weeks after returning to Damascus, I landed a job at an English-language Syrian magazine.

Every morning I'd go to the Syrian Arab News Agency's website and copy-and-paste government propaganda into our political pages. We were not to alter, add, or edit, even to fix the misspellings. We were not allowed to offer a better translation, or to write our own political news. We didn't even have to cite SANA as our source, which itself never gave the names of the journalists who wrote the articles.

Our own team consisted of five journalists, among them Essam, an older man who didn't know how to use a computer or speak English very well. Odd, for an English-language magazine. Painfully thin, with a chin that rarely saw a sharp razor, his presence made me uncomfortable. I puzzled over why he'd been hired as a reporter when he never actually wrote any reports. He'd show up late, sit in his office playing solitaire with a slow mouse, and smoke cheap local cigarettes alone on the balcony.

The only time we saw him working was in the afternoon, before the newspaper was sent to the printer. He'd turn off his computer and convene his daily meeting with our chief editor. Through the glass divider we could see our boss flipping the pages of the newspaper on his screen, explaining in detail every article to appear in the following day's edition. Essam would nod in agreement, never saying a word. Then, after his meeting, he'd collect his things and leave early. Essam was a Mukhabarat: a secret police officer assigned by Syria's Military Intelligence Directorate to oversee the production of our newspaper and ensure that we were indeed toeing the government line.

He attempted to start a conversation with me multiple times, but I'd withdraw into my work or feign an urgent need to run to the washroom. Days after my joining the team, Essam added me on Facebook. It was weird, given that I'd never seen him using a computer to access the internet before, nor did I think he even knew what Facebook was.

I decided to ask him point-blank. "Hey, you added me on social media?" He looked confused and said he wasn't sure what I was talking about.

A puppet profile, I thought. Probably overseen by his bosses to monitor the folks he worked with. All the other journalists, including the chief editor, were listed as mutual friends. I figured it was best to accept his friend request, although I made sure his access to my posts and photos was limited.

Then there was Myriam, a short-haired young woman who often wore basketball jerseys and baggy jeans to the office. Having quickly developed a camaraderie over cigarettes and cups of coffee, we partnered on articles about such things as discrimination based on colourism in Syria, tattoo artists opening businesses in a country where the art form was considered sinful, and the meanings of historic Damascene neighbourhood names. We ordered our lunches together and gossiped about Essam's apparent lack of intelligence, cornered away from all the other journalists on our team.

Myriam was unlike many of the fearful and virtuous Syrian women I knew. She didn't cover up, and she was comfortable laughing loudly in the company of men and giving big, shoulder-slapping hugs. Although I suspected she was a lesbian, Syria wasn't exactly the prime locale for a queer meet-cute. We spent weeks trying to find ways to come out to each other while remaining protected. Homosexuality was and still is punishable with three years' imprisonment in Syria, and no one wanted to be in a Syrian prison in 2011. And so we participated in what amounted to an extended game of chicken. Who would do it first? Who would lead this intense sexual orientation tango?

Finally, fed up with the guessing game, I came out to Myriam one morning during our morning coffee and cigarette break on the balcony.

"Duh," she said, as assured as ever. "What took you so long?"

"You could have come out first, you know."

"What do you mean?" Myriam looked me up and down. Had I misread the signs? Assumed too much? I was about to apologize when she finally let out a ringing laugh. "I'm joking, you dumb-dumb. Yes, I'm a lesbian."

From that moment on we were inseparable.

Most nights I sat alone on the floor of my little apartment in Damascus, smoking a joint and watching the news.

The revolution evolved differently in Syria. It did not ask for the end of the dictatorship, as it had in Tunisia and Egypt. It targeted well-known corrupt politicians and businessmen and left Bashar al-Assad untouched, almost holy in his presidential chair. In those early days, Syrians believed that it was not Al-Assad but the powerful group around him that was responsible for the country's economic and cultural decline.

I disagreed, believing that al-Assad continued his father's bloody work but simply hid it better. A master of optics, he'd traded in his father's military outfit for an Armani suit, studied medicine in London, married a well-educated blond woman, and laughed good-naturedly as he praised students and factory workers in strategic photo ops. Meanwhile across Damascus his Mukhabarat were pulling those who stood against him out of their beds at dawn and either disappearing them forever or returning them months later with broken bones and crooked minds.

"The situation in Syria is different," I posted on Facebook, maintaining the charade to the dismay of my Egyptian friends. "Syrian people believe in Bashar al-Assad. He is a good president."

Moments later, Essam's puppet profile liked my status.

Al-Assad told *The Wall Street Journal* that progress toward political reform had been slow and halting. However, he insisted that Syria would be spared from the Arab Spring wave. The Syrian government was in alignment with the Syrian people, he claimed, specifically in its anti-Western stance and its cold war against Israel.

"Other presidents in the region were not in such alignment," I posted on Facebook, rolling my eyes. "That's why they were ousted by their people."

Essam liked the post.

The demonstrations started small; revolutionaries called them flash protests. By the time you reached the protest, it was over. You'd see only its aftermath: police cars gathered; plainclothes officers exchanging suspicious looks; shop owners reopening their doors with jolty, anxious steps; maybe the echo of a distant chant.

Then the protests grew: in smaller towns around Damascus and on the outskirts of the city. People would rush out of mosques after the Friday prayers, gather with strength in numbers, and chant. Then they'd be interrupted by the wheezing of bullets and would scatter in every direction.

"Al-Assad is a reformer. He is a modern president," I wrote in a status box on Facebook, then decided against posting it and abandoned the site for a while.

Al-Assad brought back the authoritarian tactics of his late father's administration. His "reform" included pervasive censorship and surveillance and brutal violence against suspected opponents of the regime. He oversaw the restructuring of the Syrian economy from a largely communist model to a more capitalist and liberalized one. Such changes mostly served to enrich a network of businessmen with direct connections to the Assad family: his brother-in-law and many cousins.

Syrian people continued to fill the streets, chests naked to incoming bullets, chanting for freedom. The regime soldiers were told to chant back for a holy trinity: Allah, Syria, and Bashar.

March 2011 marked the first major protest in Syria, in a tiny little town called Daraa, to the south of Damascus. This rural farming centre woke up one morning to the wails of women and the howling of men. The day before, a group of school-age kids who'd heard the chants and seen the Arab Spring news on television had not only gone out chanting themselves but had also graffitied their school walls with anti-regime slogans. These children had very little knowledge of the likely consequences of their actions. They begged for their lives when the regime forces arrested them. They cried as they were tortured in the regime's dungeons. Their mothers screeched when their dead, bullet-ridden bodies were delivered back to their homes in the early hours of the next day.

The town did not sleep: every man, woman, and child took to the streets in protest. For the first time, the people called for the fall of Bashar al-Assad.

The regime forces arrested the masses. They fired at protesters. Blood pooled in the streets. Videos of the death and destruction in Daraa were shared on WhatsApp, posted anonymously on Facebook, and smuggled out of the country to foreign media. The protests echoed in small towns across Syria, and the new chant dominated: *We want the fall of Bashar.*

As the protests increased in size, the regime responded in kind: snipers were sent to Baniyas, tanks were deployed to Homs, and helicopters dropped explosive barrels onto protesters from the sky. Protesters in turn picked up arms, shooting back at regime forces. Some of the army officers, mortified by their own actions, defected, hiding out in villages or escaping the country altogether. Some of them decided to organize their own armed forces. They called themselves the Free Syrian Army.

In June 2011, months after these protests started, the people of Jisr ash-Shughūr, a Syrian town near the border with Turkey, joined the revolution. The regime responded with tanks and missiles, and soon the people of this town became the first wave of Syrian refugees to escape over the border.

One morning in late March 2011, we were told at the newspaper to finish our tasks early; then, in one big group, we were herded out of the office. Other employees from the parent media company showed up too, as well as our neighbours: nurses and administrators from the private practice next door, suited men and well-dressed women from the business centre, and children from the school. A man we didn't know handed us white T-shirts emblazoned with a black-and-white picture of the Syrian president. We were offered freshly ironed Syrian flags and white hats that came in one size, then we were told to wait.

Moments later large public transport buses showed up, and we were told to get in. As we drove to a main road the driver encouraged us to hang our Syrian flags out the windows, take photos, and post them on Facebook.

When the buses arrived at Umayyad Square in downtown Damascus, which was barricaded from cars, we disembarked and stood in the sun.

"It's a pro-regime march," Myriam said, stating the obvious.

Pro-regime marches were something I'd been doing since the age of twelve, back when they were a ploy to show support for Hafez al-Assad, our immortal leader and the dead father of our current president. Our teachers asked us to synchronize our flag waving, taught us slogans and chants, and then sent us on our merry way. We loved these days: no school, no parents, just us kids and the city of Damascus. Hafez would stand on his presidential balcony in his palace in Al-Maleki neighbourhood and wave his fists back at the children, as if reminding them who their real father was. The tradition died out after his death in 2000, but current circumstances had evidently brought it back.

At first, Myriam and I lazily stood around smoking our cigarettes. We snuck off to a nearby bar and got some drinks in to-go cups. But as the sun rose higher in the sky the chants picked up. More buses arrived. We couldn't hear each other talk anymore. People ran around like children, and we got in the spirit, too. We drunkenly waved a flag we didn't believe in while wearing T-shirts bearing the image of our dictator. We took photos and posted them online.

The crowds began to march, and we followed their lead.

"Where are we going?" I asked.

"I have no clue." Myriam laughed. We cheersed with our paper cups and kept moving. The drums, barely noticeable at first, grew louder. The drummers sang chants, encouraging us to sing along. A car with a massive picture of the president was parked on the side of the road, its open trunk full of water bottles being given out for free. A woman handed us plastic-wrapped sandwiches.

"This is for your freedom," she said, smiling. In the distance were makeshift stages erected before our arrival for camera crews, whose black lenses engulfed us all. Women ululated, men sang. Many made peace signs with their hands raised to the sky.

Myriam and I reached the top of Al-Thawra Bridge, built upon the land my family home used to occupy. We stood on its hunchback and watched the crowd expand and take over the street, a sea of white hats occasionally interrupted by the flag, red and black with green stars. Between the sun, the day drinking, and the dehydration, I was wasted. I sat on the ground and Myriam plopped down beside me.

"This is not for us," I said. "This is for them." I pointed in the direction of the American embassy. She nodded. We sat quietly for a long time. Marchers passed and gave us dirty looks, and children appeared amused to see two grownups sitting on the asphalt.

"It's a fresh cover of paint," Myriam said. "It hides, but its very existence confirms that something needs to be hidden."

"Huh?"

She stood up and extended her hand to me. "You want to go home? I can walk you to your place."

"I have a bottle of vodka with your name on it chilling in my fridge."

"Your neighbours will go mad if they see you bring a woman home."

Over the next couple of months my house in Damascus grew in popularity. Word of mouth spread through the city's gay and lesbian communities: there was a home where you were safe to be yourself, a place of gathering during these uncertain times.

I modelled it after the home I'd grown up in: Sama's. Everyone was welcome, and joy was our ethos. If Sama still lived in Damascus she would have asked these folks to call her grandmother. But she'd packed her things and moved to Turkey in early 2011, when the protests began.

The two-bedroom house sat like a cube on the outskirts of a shabby neighbourhood with roads that were dusty in summer and muddy in winter. It had been unoccupied before me, silent until I filled it with queer people. I had a bed, a closet, a TV, and a couch. The windows, up near the ceiling, afforded privacy but rarely allowed sunlight in, and the bathroom flooded every now and then. But what made it special was the fact that a queer person could walk in and take off the mask they'd put on for the society outside. Gay men gave up their performatively deep voices, wheezed with laughter, and cozied up to one another unafraid. Lesbian women took off their hijabs and rested in the arms of one another while smoking joints.

The boys monitored the streets until they were empty of eye-witnesses, then whistled for the girls to run out of cars. Inside we'd crank up the music, drink till we were drunk, and play card games into the early morning hours. Girls made excuses for one another to explain absences to their parents. The second bedroom, bare of anything but a carpet, became a safe space for lovers to excuse themselves and have sex without fear of being found.

I made copies of my key for Myriam and Omar, who made copies for their friends, who made copies for others. Soon, over forty copies graced keychains around the city, talismans of safety and community.

"You want to watch something fun?" I asked the room one night. Myriam and the other women were huddled together on the sofa. "Have you ever heard of *The Vagina Monologues*?"

I attached my laptop to the TV and played a pirated version of the HBO special. Silence fell on the room as we watched Eve Ensler recount the stories of the women she'd interviewed. Myriam teared up at the testimony of an old lady who'd never had an orgasm and laughed at the sex noises Ensler acted out on a stage.

"Do you have more of this?" someone asked when the special ended. "We should play movies like this on a regular basis!"

A weekly tradition was born. We pooled our money and bought a used projector. Every week I'd choose a queer movie and play it for those gathered in my living room. The tradition picked up, and attendance grew. I screened *The Birdcage* for a group of twenty and *In & Out* at three in the morning to thunderous laughter. I ran a *Queer as Folk* marathon, and people kept one another up to date when they missed episodes.

"We should call this the Safe Home," Myriam said one morning as she walked through the metal gate with breakfast for everyone. I held a finger up to my lips as we tiptoed through the sleeping crowd in the living room to the kitchen for coffee.

"I don't know if the name matters," I said, sleep still in my eyes. "What matters is that all these folks are sound asleep in one another's arms." We stood at the kitchen door and looked at them dozing in a pile like a litter of puppies.

"They look so peaceful," she whispered.

This wasn't always the case, of course. A fight once broke out when Omar asserted that lesbians are manly by nature.

"Your gender identity and sexual orientation are two different things," I said, parroting what I'd learned over the years from books and online research. Everyone looked to me to elaborate.

"Think about it this way. Your gender identity is who you see yourself as: a man, a woman, a trans person, et cetera." I used the commanding voice my father had taught me—firm, authoritative. "Your sexual orientation is who you're attracted to. So, gender is internal, while orientation is external."

"Okay, smartass," Myriam said from the corner of the room. "No wonder Sama called you Labibah."

"Hey, I want to hear this," another man said. He was a newcomer, a friend of a friend with a smile that showed pearly teeth. He wore a loose T-shirt that offered a glimpse of his hairy chest.

"Okay." I paused, gathered my thoughts, and continued. "There are six pillars to your sexuality."

Your biological sex, I explained, is the first pillar. It's what a doctor told your parents the day you were born. It was assigned to you at birth. It speaks to the physical appearance of what gender you were assumed to be. Your gender identity is who you think of yourself as: man, woman, or otherwise. Your sexual orientation is who you're attracted to. The fourth pillar is your gender expression: how you tie your hair, what clothes you wear, how you signify your gender outwardly to others. Another pillar is your sexual practices: what you do, or don't do, when you're in bed with someone.

"The further your sexual practices are from your gender identity and sexual orientation," I continued, "the more troubling it is for you to be fulfilled sexually."

"So, a gay man married to a woman is troubled?" the man asked.

"Well, he's forced—either by society, his family, or even himself—into a sexual practice that doesn't ring true to his identity," I said. "It's a traumatic place to be."

Everyone seemed to be chewing on what I'd said. I'm sure I had a smug little look on my face. Silently I thanked my years of obsessively trying to understand myself and those around me through Wikipedia pages, online essays, and conversations with queer foreigners in Egypt.

"What about the sixth pillar?" the man in the corner asked. "You said there were six."

"Oh, that's a fun one," I said. "It's your sexual citizenship."

I paused for effect.

"It's the way society at large sees you based on your biological sex, gender identity, sexual orientation, gender expression, and sexual practices. Where society places you in the hierarchy of its people according to these identities you carry."

A straight married man in Damascus is at the top of the hierarchical pyramid of our society, I explained. Add to that wealth, education, and a white-collar career, and you get the king of our community. We as queer men are almost at the bottom of that pyramid, right below lesbian women (whom the society looks at with less antagonism than gay men), and right above sex workers and divorced women.

"Danny, you're drunk." Myriam said. "Did you just come up with this on the spot?"

We laughed, and my lecture seemed to have reached its logical end. We went back to downing our drinks and smoking our joints. I pulled out the joystick of my trusted PlayStation and we played a couple rounds of Mortal Kombat. Omar took a corner with the woman he'd offended with his comment, and the two conversed intensely. I sat on the floor, held the argileh handle, and pushed soft purple clouds of smoke out of my lungs.

I felt a warm hand on my shoulder. It was the man with the hairy chest. Without a word he extended his hand to me; I stood up. He pulled me to the bedroom, and as soon as the door closed behind us, he kissed me. I squeezed his slender body between my arms and heard him moan. People outside cheered, as they often did when a match was made.

An hour later we were naked, sweaty, and entwined on the carpet. He rested his head on my chest and smiled.

"So," he said, "tell me more about these six pillars of yours."

VIRAL

"Do you know Amina Arraf?"

Yet another email from yet another journalist had landed in my inbox. Everyone was talking about Amina, the person behind the Gay Girl in Damascus blog. The hashtag #FreeAmina had gone extremely viral, and people across the world were now demanding her release.

We at the Safe Home learned of Amina the same way the rest of the world had: through her blog posts. We'd talked about her in one of our Sunday meetings, which by then had been going strong for months. We had dedicated Tuesdays for queer movie nights, Thursdays for discussing social issues, Fridays for our weekly party, and Saturdays for card games and backgammon championships. Mondays and Wednesdays were my days off. The neighbours, clocking the mix of women and men entering and leaving the house, must have assumed we were having a gay ol' heterosexual time. Sometimes they knocked, angry-faced, pointy-fingered, threatening to call the police, but we knew that no one would be calling the police in this time of civil unrest. Still, for safety, we developed a secret knock to the tune of Coldplay's "Paradise."

We also started a private Facebook group for the Safe Home, which grew in membership from a dozen people to over four thousand. Most of these had puppet accounts with cartoon profile photos and fake names, but all had to be recommended by a fellow member who knew them in real life before they could be admitted to the virtual group.

"Anyone know who this Amina person is?" I asked in one of our gatherings, weeks before Amina's arrest. We knew the name was fake. Arraf is not a familiar Syrian last name, and Amina was so old-fashioned.

"It's weird that none of us have met or even heard of her," Myriam said.

"She says she was educated in North America," Omar said. "Maybe that explains the lack of connection to the community?"

Amina's latest post, "My Father, the Hero," had raised some suspicions among us. In it, she narrated the early morning knock on her family home's door, police officers showing up to arrest her, and her father—a well-educated and loving man who accepted her and her sexuality—defending her. He managed, according to the post, to lecture the police officers away, saving her from arrest.

"This is bullshit," I said.

We were gathered in the living room, probably smoking weed and drinking. Someone was likely preoccupied with the PlayStation, and perhaps folks were taking advantage of the room next door. Our community had grown and the atmosphere had flourished. An artsy gay man had drawn flowers on one of the walls with chalk and paint. A lesbian had asked us to write all the insults hurled at us online and in real life onto Post-it notes, which she collected and stuck to a piece of poster board cut into the shape of a heart; we hung it over the bed. Someone bought candles to create ambient mood lighting for romantic evenings. When we found another couch, abandoned on a street corner, four of us carried it into the living room and then some of us restitched it with fabric patches.

"This woman has an active imagination," someone said. "Is she even really gay?"

"Well, she was interviewed by *The Guardian*," I said. "Hailed as a beacon of hope in Damascus."

We laughed, passed a joint around. Maybe someone moaned in the next room, making us laugh even harder.

"No one escapes a morning-hour arrest," Omar said. "If her father defended her, they would have arrested him too."

"She's just writing fiction. She wrote poetry on that blog before." Myriam handed me the joint. "Let her express herself. We shouldn't be in the business of telling people how to live their lives."

"Yeah," I mused. "But she brings a lot of the regime's attention to the LGBT community in Syria. They've left us alone for years now. We don't need the focus back on us."

Weeks later, we woke to the news that Amina had been arrested by the Syrian regime. The blog post was written by Amina's cousin and claimed that she'd been apprehended in a bus station on her way to a revolutionary meeting.

The news jolted our community. The number of members in our Facebook group suddenly dropped by the hundreds. Attendance at our weekly activities dwindled.

"Where are all the people?" I asked Myriam. We were sitting in the living room, cueing up a pirated version of *Black Swan* on the projector.

"Everyone is afraid," she said.

Every foreign journalist in the Middle East wanted to cover the story. My inbox was overflowing with messages from people I hadn't spoken to in years asking for information about a woman I'd never met. Journalists never take no for an answer; when I got back to them with the fact that I'd never met the woman, they'd ask me to dig around for them. When I said it was too hard to find information in Syria, they'd beg, plead, and remind me of the good times we shared in Cairo. Finally I gave in and put a call out in the Facebook group for anyone with any information on Amina's whereabouts.

"It's clearly a fake name, but she must have had friends. She talks about the community all the time in her posts," I wrote, attaching a couple of screenshots of photos she'd posted on her blog.

Slowly the replies trickled in, a common thread uniting them. No one had ever seen this woman. No other lesbian woman in Damascus, in the thousands we were directly connected to, had ever met her for coffee or a hookup. If this woman lived in Damascus, she was celibate.

The internet pressure grew. A picture of Amina—short hair, a birthmark on her right cheek—was turned into a black-and-white emblem, and profile pictures of selfies and smiles were replaced with a poster demanding her freedom. Tweets were retweeted, and long Facebook posts from those triggered by the news were widely shared.

In the back of my mind I killed the thought that it was all too theatrical. But certain things didn't add up. A gay girl in Damascus who publicly posted her face but had to change her name. An identity she kept secret even from her long-distance girlfriend in Canada, whom she never saw face to face, even though Skype was available in Syria. A father who accepted his daughter's homosexuality, capable of fending off regime forces out for her arrest. A forced disappearance on her way to plan a revolution. It was all very epic, like a Greek mythology heroine fated with punishment by her gods and admiration from her people.

"Hey, can we meet for coffee?" I texted Majd, an old fling, a ranked officer in the Syrian Army whom I knew from my days at the internet café, back when he was a new army recruit.

"Sure," he shot back. "Should I come to your house?"

"Can we meet in a café? I have a couple of questions for you."

"Sure! But can we go to your house after?" He sent a winky-face. I rolled my eyes; some things never change.

We sat in the sunlight outside a café on the Mezzeh highway. The humidity hadn't sunk in yet; the June sun was gentle until three in the afternoon, when it turned the old city into an oven. The smell of chlorine from the nearby public pool filled our noses. Majd wore plainclothes; he'd gained weight around the waist and lost some of his lush hair in the years since I'd seen him.

"Do you still live with Sama?" he asked.

"Mother packed her bags and fled to Turkey months ago," I said. "She lives in Istanbul now."

"She's not made for conflict, that one."

"No, she's had enough drama in her life," I joked. "She kissed me on the forehead and got in her car and drove off."

"That's a long drive," he said.

"Days at least."

I leaned toward him. He leaned in, too, probably thinking I was about to murmur something naughty in his ear.

"Do you know Amina Arraf?" I whispered.

"Who?" he jolted his head back.

"The blogger?"

"What blogger?"

"The gay girl in Damascus."

He shushed me, leaned back in, and asked me to elaborate. I relayed the story and asked him if he could find out whether she had indeed been arrested. "The regime must keep a list or something. Maybe it's on a computer somewhere? Can you access it?"

"We don't arrest civilians," Majd said, flatly reciting the regime's line.

"And you're also straight," I said. "Now can we cut the bullshit?"

He took a sip of his coffee, then locked eyes with me. "Why do you need to know? If she was arrested, she's gone. These prisons are no place for women, let alone lesbians."

"I need to know, okay?" Even I didn't know why. "There's something strange about this whole thing."

Finally he nodded and promised to see what he could do.

That evening, I sent Omar a cryptic text we both knew how to decipher. He'd been working on the down-low with revolutionary committees, helping design their social media posters.

"Hey, are you still with the boys?" I said, referring to his contacts on the anti-regime side.

"Yeah, we're meeting tomorrow. What's up?"

"I need you to ask them something. There's this cousin of mine who went on a holiday to her aunt's home. We haven't heard from her since. She was supposed to be hanging out with the boys but had to cut her visit short."

An *aunt's home* is code in Syria for the prisons of the Mukhabarat police.

"Can you ask the boys if anyone met her before her visit to her aunt's home?"

"Are you trying to go visit her there, too?" he asked.

"No. I'll be fine. I just need to know if anyone knew where she went."

By the next day I'd gathered all the information I needed. Majd confirmed that there was no record of the arrest described in the blog post. Omar confirmed that the rebels' Local Coordination Committee in Damascus had never met or heard of Amina Arraf.

I went on Twitter and DMed Andy Carvin, an NPR journalist who followed me back.

"Andy, Amina Arraf is not a real person."

I didn't yet know if the person behind the account was a man or a woman or even Syrian. But I knew in my gut that Amina Arraf was a character, a facade.

"I have from a good source that she is indeed real," he wrote. "We'll see, though."

"I just needed to tell someone. This madness is bringing too much attention to LGBTQ people, and it might eff us up."

A week later, Andy worked with lesbian author and blogger Liz Henry and an online Chicago-based news publication to uncover the truth. They used hackers, online investigators, and website data mining to pinpoint the location from which Amina's posts were generated: an unassuming single-family home in Scotland, owned by an American man named Tom MacMaster.

The BBC had a revelation of their own. They found the woman whose photos had been used to portray Amina: a Ukrainian immigrant in the U.K. who'd never been to Syria and had very little knowledge of the situation there.

At first, Tom MacMaster denied being the creator behind Amina Arraf. He insisted that journalists were unfairly targeting him, showing up at his doorstep, spreading rumours about him. A couple of days later, though, he came clean on the Gay Girl in Damascus blog. He deleted all his posts and shared a short apology stating that he'd meant no harm.

MacMaster had visited Syria with his wife back in the early 2000s and later created the character of Amina as an online experiment. He used it to write lesbian erotic poetry, to chat with other lesbians on online forums, and form online sexual relationships with unsuspecting women across the globe.

When asked why he'd impersonated a brown queer woman to report on the revolution in Syria, he denied that it was all for his sexual gratification. He stated that his voice wouldn't have been heard otherwise. "When all the attention came, I thought here is an opportunity to put forward some things I thought were important: issues around Middle East conflict, religious subjects," MacMaster said in an interview with *The Washington Post*. "However, I also had a real ego boost in thinking that, 'I'm good. I'm smart. These journalists don't realize I'm punking them.'"

During the period in which he managed to punk the journalists, MacMaster answered interview questions on behalf of Amina for *The Guardian* and *The Washington Post*. Articles were written about his creation, hailing it as a perfect example of the modern revolution in Syria.

On the day he claimed that his persona was arrested, over two hundred and fifty civilians actually were arrested in Syria. None of them had an international campaign for their release. Nor did the over two hundred thousand Syrians the regime forcefully disappeared after that.

"I feel really awful about the fact that the Syrian government has been claiming that the Western government is making up stories, and now they can use me as evidence," MacMaster added.

Meanwhile, on local channels in Syria, the story of Amina Arraf became a pastime for pro-regime propaganda machines. "Look at the Western imperialist countries trying to control Syria," a pro-Assad presenter proclaimed. "They want to bring the abnormality of homosexuality to our pure country, and they use the internet to scam you with Western values."

Over the next few months, our usual hangout places in Damascus were patrolled extensively. The government knew of our gatherings but had looked the other way for years. After Amina, we noticed police cars touring the parks and streets we frequented. Plainclothes officers awkwardly walked around, examining everyone they passed. Nightclubs that used to allow us the freedom to dance together shut their doors to us. Neighbours shouted religious prayers at us when we walked out to buy groceries. We awoke to find a car window had been smashed overnight.

It all came to a head when, in late 2011, months after the story of Amina broke, a neighbour caught Myriam, Omar, and me sneaking back into the Safe Home together. She screamed at us from afar, and her screams attracted more neighbours.

We quickly went inside, but the neighbours gathered outside the gate and continued to shout. A man said he'd bring his gun next time. A woman yelled that we brought them shame. They called us infidels, deviants, and dogs. We huddled in the kitchen, unsure of our next move.

"Maybe we should chill out for a bit," Myriam posted on our Facebook group. "Maybe we shouldn't meet up in the home for a while." The post gathered a lot of likes, and for months the Safe Home was deserted. I slept on couches and in the backseat of Myriam's car. I snuck in every once in a while, making sure not to turn on lights. The house returned to being cold and dirty, and I never managed to have a good night's sleep there after that.

We hung out in cars, driving around town, drinking in the backseats, finding coves in the mountains around Damascus and smoking weed behind rocks. No more conversations about the six pillars of sexuality, no more movie nights. No more moans from the neighbouring room or sweaty naked bodies pressed up against mine. We were closed for business, waiting for the storm to pass.

I didn't know how to put it into words back then, but I now understand that this was an intensely racist and homophobic hoax.

This straight white man, living a comfortable life in Europe, decided to adopt the persona of a queer woman of colour in order to gain power in a place where he had no business taking space. His actions led to an increase in surveillance upon the community he impersonated. They had a serious effect on my own life and on the lives of people around me. To top it off, his actions went unpunished. He was a media pariah for a week or two, then slowly his story faded, lost among the dozens of other stories coming out of the Middle East, occupying a tiny little space of the international consciousness.

Did he sit at home and plan all this with racism in mind? I don't think so. Very few people wake up in the morning and decide to be actively racist. But he did act from a place of privilege afforded him by his whiteness. He acted from a place of safety afforded him by the systemic racism that gave him this freedom and that didn't feel the need to punish him for his deeds.

In one of my interviews following the revelation of this hoax, I said that I wished I lived in a country where I could sue him. I wished to see him face the consequences of his actions and pay for what he did to my community.

To this day I still find comments from puppet accounts on articles I write and on reviews of my books. The commenters question whether I'm a real person, whether I faked my Syrian identity like Tom MacMaster.

I don't want to give MacMaster undue importance: he's but a sad, lonely man with a sexual kink. His actions, however, had repercussions that continue to this day.

In early 2012 I moved into a different house with a new set of gay roommates. Slowly, members dropped out of our Safe Home circle, one after the other. Some immigrated to Lebanon or Turkey, others retreated into different corners of the city. And some—like Myriam—found new love and became consumed by their own private dramas.

I, on the other hand, dated an employee at the Brazilian embassy in Damascus. But dating, as was always the case with me back then, is a stretch. We fucked regularly. I had very little interest in a committed relationship. I played it cool and buried my feelings deep, because I knew that if I were to be vulnerable with someone, the floodgates would open and all my emotional damage from the past years would pour out with the strength of the Nile.

The man, tall and handsome with a beard as black as night, invited me for a drink with his colleagues in a fancy café overlooking the city. I arrived late so as not to appear eager and joined the table of eight, picking a spot a couple seats down from the Brazilian.

The woman I sat beside introduced herself as Liz and seemed unusually interested in me. She had blond hair, blue eyes, and a British accent, which I always found endearing. Eventually she explained her interest: she was a journalist for *The Washington Post*, and I was the only non-foreigner at the table.

Guarded at first, we discussed the current political climate: the regime's attacks on troubling towns, the siege of Homs, the intensifying refugee crisis, and the Free Syrian Army. She asked if I was worried about the Islamic State of Iraq and Syria that was forming on our borders.

"The Syrian president released the Islamic extremists his father kept in Syrian prisons for years," I said. "It's a smart strategic move on his part. He created his own enemy in the image that scares the West the most: an extremist Islamic terrorist group."

I looked around as the others at the table chatted away. Bottles of prosecco popped. The Brazilian flashed me a smile.

"Of course I'm afraid of ISIS," I continued. "What I'm more afraid of is that the world will be so scared of ISIS that it will see Assad as the lesser of two evils."

She asked whether I was on Twitter, and I directed her to my account. "Oh. That's insane," she said.

"What?"

She pointed to my profile, which I operated under a fake name at the time, and asked if I was really this person.

"Of course," I said. "I can tweet something for you right now, if you'd like."

"We thought you were another of MacMaster's puppets or a government bot," she explained. "We had a bet about you in our Beirut office."

"Well, I'm a real boy!" I mimicked in a Pinocchio singsong.

She handed me a business card with *The Washington Post* logo on it. "If you're ever in Beirut, let me know."

The handsome Brazilian and I broke things off a few days later, and I forgot all about Liz Sly, the head of the *Post*'s bureau in Beirut, until the day I was arrested in Syria.

DEPARTURE (1)

I am losing the streets of Damascus.

It is not a sudden loss, like a severed limb. Nor is it a persistent ache, like a broken rib in need of readjustment. It's mostly an after-thought. It comes and goes as it pleases and catches me, unprepared, when I'm knee-deep in the mundane. It flashes uninvited and consumes all my senses, then disappears. I feel it in my belly, an echo of laughter at a joke I don't recall. I feel it on my lips, a phantom kiss from a foreign mouth. I taste it on my tongue, a spice with an Arabic name that escapes me. Then, as soon as I steady my wandering mind, it goes away.

I write this at my desk with a view of Vancouver. I respond to emails, message with friends, and rage-tweet at the world. Then suddenly time folds in on itself and I'm in the heart of Damascus. The memory is no match for the real thing. It's a screenshot of a home movie. Sometimes it's clearer: the street I grew up on, the corner store where I used to buy smokes. More often, though, it's blurry, as if the memory itself is uncertain why it was pulled from the depth of my subconscious.

A short-circuit in the brain, I think, and try to let it go.

But the memory demands investigation, with very few clues and no motive. What was that street called again? Did I live on the sixth floor of that building or the seventh? What brand of cigarettes did I buy at the corner store? Was the cute cashier tall or short? Did his touch linger when he handed me my change? Did we kiss? I think we kissed.

I search old photos taken in Damascus for stable backgrounds and faces of people whose names I can't recall. But the photos are mostly indoors, rarely of the streets. Taking a photo in a Damascene street attracts the eyes of passersby, some of whom could be government informants bent on blocking photographic evidence that the city lives and breathes.

I go to Google Maps and search Damascus. I try to select Street View, but no Google employee was ever permitted to pass through with their film equipment. The streets are lines on a map, never straight, always twirling like a dervish around historic buildings. I remember either their names or their facades, but never both.

The Safe Home no longer exists. The Syrian government got tired of the district, where many rebel fighters found refuge and passage, and bulldozed it to the ground. I dare you to search it on Google Maps right now. Type *Basateen el-Razi* into the search field and switch to satellite view. See the land emptied of homes, replaced by a triangle of yellow desert. It's clearly manmade, surgical and intentional. But Google Maps remembers the streets that used to be there before the homes were bulldozed. There are imaginary lines on the map showing where these streets used to be, like veins on a corpse.

I trace the memories on my body. My aches are my keys. My broken rib—the fourth on the left—that cracked under the heavy boots of a uniformed officer. The fracture is right in the middle of the intercostal space, in the bone between the costal cartilage and the base of the scapula. It aches when it rains, memory strumming my ribcage like guitar strings. X-rays show that after breaking, it fused back in a semi-crooked way. It looks like a hem made by a sewing machine. If only I could undo it by pulling the thread, rebuild it to my satisfaction. The doctors tell me that the only way to fix it would be to insert a rod between my ribs and open up my ribcage like theatre curtains. It's not worth it, they insist, and I agree with them, until it rains.

●

Here is what I remember:

The door opened, and the same officer who broke my rib asked me to follow him. I lifted my tired body off the dusty floor and obeyed.

We walked down a long hallway, with offices on both sides. I heard laughter and hushed conversations behind closed doors, and through open ones I saw officers hunched over paperwork. None of the rooms had windows. I assumed we were underground.

The hallway curved. Around the corner appeared a body on the floor, as if placed there for shock value. Shirtless and slumped on his side, the man was covered in bruises. The only sign that he might be alive was a stream of blood oozing from his nose. The officer escorting me stepped over him, almost inconvenienced by the body, while I stood staring.

"Hurry up!" he demanded. I squeezed against the wall and tried my best not to step over the man. The officer watched me squirm.

Finally he opened a door and pushed me in by the shoulder. Inside the well-lit room was an older officer in a full military outfit sitting behind the desk. He had a fan directed at his sweating face and his shirt buttons were undone down to the middle of his chest, allowing a bush of white hair to peek through. He gestured for me to sit on the plastic chair in front of him.

The fan rasped. His pen made a scratching noise. A clock hanging over the door clicked off beat. On the wall over his head a giant photo of Bashar al-Assad, looking pensively toward the future, crowned the otherwise empty office. The officer picked his nose almost compulsively.

He looked up from his papers. "What's your name?"

"Ahmad Ramadan, sir," I said.

"Ahmad?"

"Ahmad Ramadan, sir."

He pulled a folder from the piles on his desk, opened it, flipped its pages, then returned his eyes to me. He asked me for my parents' names and my date of birth. I answered quietly. He returned to his papers, then exhaled in frustration.

"Do you know a Danny Ramadan?" he asked.

"No, sir."

"Maybe a distant cousin, or a half brother?"

"No, sir. The name is not familiar, sir."

"Maybe we will bring your mother here and ask her ourselves, maybe she would remember."

Good luck with that, I thought, but didn't dare say it. I remained silent and gazed at the floor. Moments passed. Thinking he'd returned to his papers, I looked up only to find him still eyeing me.

"Maybe if you have a picture, sir? Maybe that would help?" I asked, gambling for information.

"We don't have a picture," he said. Silence returned to the room. The cold tiles felt nice on my swollen feet. Two officers had come to my cell a couple of nights before, singling me out in the crowded room and pushing me against the corner. Mouth dry, lips cracking, no water or fresh air for what felt like a week, I asked in a raspy voice what they wanted as they turned me around to face the wall.

The room, occupied by two dozen prisoners, was eerily silent. The only thing I could hear was the rustling behind me. The first kick jolted my lower back. My face smacked against the wall.

"Just tell me what you want." I tried to turn around but found myself on the floor. One of them grabbed my legs and held them up high while the other slapped the soles of my feet repeatedly with a long bendy cable. I screamed; the cable whipped like a young tree branch snapping back at you. After a while I stopped screaming, but I ached with every lash.

The other prisoners moved to the opposite side of the cell, gathered silently in a corner, and watched. It wasn't the first time an officer or two had appeared, picked a prisoner seemingly at random, inflicted pain for no apparent reason, then walked out. Eventually the one holding up my legs dropped them, then kicked the side of my chest. I heard the bone crack. Then they left the room.

A couple of fellow prisoners walked over, grabbed me from under the armpits, and carried me to the wall. They told me to rest my back on its cold tiles.

It took me a second to realize I had peed myself.

"If you tell me what I need to know," the old officer said now, "you'll be released in no time."

"I am sorry, sir," I said. "I wish I could help."

I said only enough to keep the conversation going, and I avoided eye contact. I hunched forward, squeezed my chest between my arms, and leaned in upon myself in the chair.

"You grew up with an unpredictable adult," my therapist would say years later. "You had to be attuned to her ups and downs, and to monitor your situation at all times for your own safety. You've learned how to read people and give them the right responses to ease their discomfort. You were trained for this since the day you were born. In a way, your childhood trauma saved your life."

I sat quietly before the military officer, who returned to his paperwork and ignored me for hours. Every now and then a young soldier would come in, pass him papers, whisper in his ear, or hand him a walkie-talkie that he'd speak into in short sentences. My chest ached, but I did not relax in my seat. My bladder demanded relief, but I kept quiet. Finally he looked at me, seemingly surprised I was still there. He called for his assistant to come in and return me to my cell.

On my way back I saw that the near-dead body was gone; a trail of blood led to one of the many rooms with closed doors down the hall. We arrived at my cell and the officer shoved me back in. My cellmates' eyes squinted in the sudden light. I took in as many of the faces as I could before the doors closed again and returned us to darkness.

◆

A week or two earlier, my life had been heading in a completely different direction.

In May 2012 I was invited by a prestigious university in Jordan to deliver a talk about my two short-story collections and to partner with an American author on a translation project. The four-day trip wasn't out of the ordinary for me: by then, my books had amassed a good following in the Middle East. And my Twitter account—still under a fake name—was gaining momentum.

I also began to gain favour with foreign publications. Under a pseudonym, I wrote articles for *Foreign Policy* and *The Guardian* and was quoted regularly in other news outlets. On Twitter I reported on the protests, fights, and explosions that were now occurring on a weekly basis.

On my way to Amman, I was stopped at the airport by a border guard.

The man, sitting behind a glass partition, checked my passport multiple times and asked more questions than usual. I named my parents and cousins and then stepped aside so that he could take a good look at me. He released me to fly to Amman.

Maybe I should have seen the sign. Maybe I shouldn't have flown back.

After a successful work week in Amman, I returned to Damascus on a late flight. I walked the old hallways of Damascus International Airport, which hadn't been updated since the early eighties, then got in line with all the other passengers waiting to be admitted into the country.

"Did you finish your military service?" the border guard asked.

"I'm the only son to my mother," I answered, indicating that I was exempt.

The guard flipped through my passport, examining its multiple visas and arrival stamps. Egypt, Turkey, Lebanon, Tunisia, and Malaysia. He went back to his computer screen, then flipped the pages of the passport some more. The folks in line behind me shuffled in place waiting for their turn.

"What's your father's name again?" he asked.

"Abdul-Kader."

He asked me to step out of the line, stand in a corner, and wait. He did not return my passport. My chest tensed as I walked to the designated corner. I looked around for exit signs but didn't see any. *Maybe I should run*, I thought, but wasn't sure where to. Many officers stood nearby with guns on their waists. The airport loudspeaker echoed in my ears and my vision tunnelled. It became almost impossible to take a breath in. I tried to steady myself but failed.

"Walk with me," the officer said. I followed him to a door and he ushered me in. I asked him where we were going.

"Don't worry. It's a routine check." We walked down a long hallway with only one door at its end and entered to find an officer behind a desk holding my passport.

"What's your name?" he asked.

"Ahmad Ramadan, sir."

The officer asked me to name all my cousins on my father's side. I did. He asked me to repeat them. I did.

"Do you have a cellphone?" he extended his palm, already knowing the answer. I dropped my phone in his hand, scanning its contents in my head. I kept no trace of work-related stuff on my phone—no Twitter access, no English-language articles—but in my contacts I did have the phone numbers of all the queer folks I knew.

"Unlock it," he said.

"It's not locked."

He bound my passport and phone together with a rubber band from his desk and told me to wait outside.

For the next four hours or so, I sat outside his door. Two more men were walked in and later joined me. We did not talk and avoided eye contact.

Finally the officer walked out accompanied by two guards. He handed a passport and a phone to one of the men and told him he could leave. He pointed to me and the other man. "The two of you are with me."

"Sir, my wife is waiting for me outside," the man pleaded. "I haven't done anything wrong."

The officer ignored him. The guards put handcuffs on us. I didn't protest. I silently walked as they paraded us out through the arrivals hall.

"I have done nothing wrong," my fellow prisoner repeated in a panicked voice.

"Shut up, you animal," one of the guards said.

"Can you tell my wife? She's outside the airport," he begged.

The slap on the back of his neck landed louder than expected. The same kind of slap my father had called airplanes. People in the customs lines stared for a second, then pretended not to notice. The man went silent.

We walked through another unmarked door, down more empty hallways, and then found ourselves outside, where a white van was waiting for us. I looked up at the May night sky.

It would be the last time I'd see the sky for the next six weeks.

●

I am going to take a moment here to ask you: What do you expect me to write about my six weeks in a Syrian dungeon? What more can I offer that might make this story worthy of your time?

Writing about this experience wouldn't ease it for me, and reading about it wouldn't validate this book for you. Would a detailed description of the physical and emotional abuse I experienced make this story more complete? Would it make me more worthy of your pity, your sympathy? Or confirm the false dichotomy that Syria is bad and Canada is good? It's easy to paint the world in black and white, to navigate life in absolutes.

In one of my latest speaking engagements, I stood six feet apart from a group of locals at a writer's residency and smiled while introducing myself. I joked, as I always do, throwing in a couple of tried-and-tested one-liners. The crowd laughed, and some even clapped in amusement. Then the facilitator opened the floor for a Q&A.

"I just don't understand," someone asked from the back of the room. "How can you be so happy?" I sighed and looked to the moderator, who didn't seem bothered by the question. The crowd eagerly awaited a response.

"I could stand here and talk to you about my trauma," I began, my voice stern. "I can fall apart onstage and spend days picking up the pieces for your entertainment. I can confirm all your assumptions. But then you'll have to pay my therapy bill."

Everyone laughed.

"It's easy for me to confirm what you think I went through, but instead I'll tell you this: I once got high with my friends in Beirut, sat on the edge of a window overlooking the city, legs dangling out, and watched the sunrise colour our home red. Was that dangerous and dumb? Yes, but it's also a happy memory. I feel the warmth of the sun on my face when I tell that story. I feel the embrace of my friends. My past is complex, and I have accepted that. Can you do the same?"

Silence fell upon the room.

What I suspect this audience member meant was that I did not look traumatized. I did not stutter or shake or cry when I talked about Syria. I fluently spoke a language I wasn't born to speak; I took up space with an authority I wasn't afforded by the colour of my skin. I defeated a stereotype that feels foreign to who I am, and it makes me feel powerful.

In my speeches and interviews I breeze through the mention of my arrest. I say it bluntly: I was arrested for six weeks by the Syrian regime, then I became a refugee in Lebanon. Curiosity flickers in the eyes of my audience, and they wait for the platter of trauma to be served. I reject that expectation and move on to the next story. When pressed by overzealous journalists, I set a clear boundary and say that I don't care to talk about it. I feel there is a right to privacy that

I should own, a right to self-determination around what you get to see of me and what I keep to myself. It's an honest answer to an overwhelming question. It's within my rights to reject it and to be a happy Syrian.

You and I talked about trust in the opening pages of this book. I promised to trust you with my stories, and you promised to trust me in my telling. Here I am, trusting you with what I've told you so far. Am I betraying this trust by not detailing more of the bloody moments I care nothing to share? Are you disappointed? Is there a value to the nights I spent cornered in a cell with a dozen or so other prisoners? Is there meaning to be distilled from the cigarette burn on my side or the permanent scar on my left foot? Counting my wounds won't bring you enlightenment. I doubt I am denying you a truth that would enhance your understanding of my experience.

I understand my responsibility as a memoirist to excavate the past and bring you pearls of wisdom from my lived experience. I take this responsibility seriously, and I am telling you—there is no more value to what I can tell you, only harm.

You have been a good reader to me. You have turned these pages and trodden softly between my words. For that, I am thankful. I ask you now to trust me that I have uncovered enough. To believe that I have written and rewritten this chapter countless times until I found the right balance between what I can tell and what I must keep to myself. Trust my silence as you've trusted my voice. This is as far as I can go.

Omar and the others worked outside while I remained inside.

Phone calls were made. Money was raised. Government officials were bribed, and my release was foretold. Six weeks later I stood in the same office I'd been questioned in. My hair and beard had grown longer than they'd ever been. I'd bitten my nails, leaving uneven edges. The officer handed me my dead phone and my passport and told me that today was the day of my release.

"Sit down," he said, gesturing to a seat. "Do you want some coffee?"

I hadn't had coffee in weeks. Since my arrest I'd lost at least thirty pounds. It hurt to sit down, but I sat nonetheless. I nodded.

"Before you leave I need to tell you a couple of things," the officer said. "Your name will be on our lists for a while. You won't be able to exit your neighbourhood. Every checkpoint will send you back in."

He asked me if I understood; I nodded. I was on house arrest. He opened his desk drawer, pulled out a business card, and handed it to me. It was white, with only a phone number on it. "How long of a while this will be is up to you," he said.

"If you see something you think is of interest to us, call and let us know. You need to show us that we can trust you. When we trust you, you will see doors opened for you, and guards at checkpoints will let you pass through."

My side ached. I wouldn't know till weeks later that a rib was broken, and that it had already healed, leaving a bone knot that I could feel under my left pec. The officer noticed and opened a small fridge behind him, pulled out an ice pack, and handed it to me. "Press it against your side," he instructed. The cold felt good on my body.

"Can I rely on you, Ahmad?" he asked, then smiled. His teeth were crooked and dark. He was missing a left incisor, making his canines look longer and sharper. The sight unexpectedly made my heart jump.

"Ahmad?" he asked again.

"Of course, you can rely on me for sure, sir." My voice quavered.

Outside, the sunlight was blinding. The metal gate closed behind me and I was left on the sidewalk, dead phone and passport in my hand.

"Danny!" I heard Omar's voice and saw him waving at me from a parked car. I must have looked like a yeti, my hair wild and uncombed, wearing the same clothes I'd been arrested in, now dirty and stained.

He gave me a bear hug, and I moaned. "I'm sorry. I'm so sorry." He looked down, and I realized I was still barefoot. His hand squeezed mine as he led me to the car and eased me into the passenger seat.

It felt as if we were driving through a tunnel. Outside the buildings bent over us and the bodies of pedestrians stretched and curved. Every honk made me jump. I flinched when Omar put a hand on my thigh. When we stopped at a traffic light, the people crossing the street stared through the windshield at me. I reclined my seat.

"I want to go home," I said when the car started moving.

"No. We all agreed that you'll stay with me for a couple nights," he said.

"I need my stuff from my home," I insisted.

"What stuff?" he asked.

"All of my stuff."

The car gained speed and I pulled my seat back up. On the streets around us boys in colourful T-shirts and girls in hijabs filtered out of high schools. People gathered around tables in cafés and restaurants.

Music emanated from a flower shop and a woman carried on a loud conversation with her children. Overwhelmed by the city's reverberations, I leaned forward and held my head between my knees.

"Danny?"

"Just take me home." I took a deep breath, straightened my back, and sat tall in my seat.

Omar drove out of the city's centre. We were stopped at multiple checkpoints along the way, but we passed through easily. I assumed the computer system hadn't yet been updated with the latest list of names to be banned and denied.

"Soon I won't be able to pass a checkpoint," I whispered.

"What? Why?" Omar asked. I shook my head. He took the highway to the neighbourhood where I'd moved.

"There were fights between the rebels and the government in the neighbourhood last week," he said. "There were tanks and explosions."

The neighbourhood was quiet, almost abandoned, save for one or two cars. The empty streets looked as though an army of city workers had come the night before and made them squeaky clean. All the shops were closed. Their metal gates looked freshly painted, suspiciously scrubbed of graffiti. A couple of curtains lifted, mistrustful eyes following our car as we pulled up to my building.

"What are we doing here?" Omar asked.

"I need to pack all my things," I said.

"Why?"

"I'm leaving."

"To my house, yes. I'm sure you can pack some clothes for now, and then—"

"No," I said. "I'm leaving for Lebanon. I'm never coming back."

Omar put the car in park and turned to face me. I told him what the officer had told me: I had mere hours before the computer systems around Damascus were updated and I was blacklisted. The only way for me to be free would be to spy on my own community. "I need to get out of here as soon as possible," I said.

"You're in pain. Don't make rash decisions," he said weakly.

"What other option do I have?"

Four hours later, I was in a taxi on my way to Beirut.

REFUGE

The United Nations High Commissioner for Refugees officer held up a slip of paper.

"You wait until someone calls the numbers in your range," she explained through a window protected by bars, sliding the paper through a narrow gap between them.

"How long is the wait?" I asked.

"How should I know?"

I was pushed aside by the person behind me in line. I texted Liz Sly, my boss at *The Washington Post* bureau in Beirut, that I'd probably be late for work. The makeshift UNHCR centre used its parking lot as a waiting area for Syrian refugees. Hundreds of men and women gathered in the open air like cursing birds forced to share a lone tree. The late-summer sun rose higher and the shaded areas became limited. I sat, eyes on the door where an officer appeared every now and then to announce a short range of numbers and then check each person's card. A simple calculation in my head informed me that I'd probably be here all day and still not make it in.

I hadn't wanted to register at the UNHCR and be acknowledged as one of the Syrian refugees in Lebanon. By mid-2012 nearly one million Syrians had crossed the border to Lebanon either legally or illegally. Most of them were placed in refugee camps in the Beqaa Valley, while a select group—the younger, more highly educated crowd—continued down to Beirut. But the UNHCR hadn't thought to build a location closer to the valley, so all refugees had to first make the day trip to the Lebanese capital. Nor was registration legally binding, given that Lebanon had rejected the request to acknowledge the Syrians as refugees, fearing the responsibilities that came with such a designation. The government had agreed only to name us as displaced citizens, as if we were someone's keys or a television remote wedged between couch cushions. This rendered the registration useless; no health benefits, meaningful support, or clear resettlement plans were ever offered.

I'd entered the country a few months ago on a tourist visa that I planned to renew every six months. However, with crimes against Syrian nationals increasing, and a viral social media post about a certain Lebanese group kidnapping Syrians in Beirut and then releasing them back inside the Syrian territories, Liz had insisted I register.

"What would that do?" I asked, but I didn't get a straight answer.

As expected, the day went by and my number wasn't called. The officer came out and instructed us to return tomorrow. "Keep your numbers!" he shouted without a mic. People shushed one another so that they could hear. "You'll be in first thing tomorrow morning."

I updated Liz. My phone rang moments later.

"Tell me how it went," she said.

"I waited for hours, then they told me to come back tomorrow."

"A good journalist keeps his eyes peeled, Danny. Remember these details. They might be good for a story one day, if we ever do a profile on the UNHCR."

I told her I'd write her an email with what I recalled from the day.

"You can of course take tomorrow off for this," she said. "Just do the news round before you head out, and text me when you're done."

The next morning I arrived at the parking lot as early as humanly possible and still found a massive line ahead of me. The doors wouldn't open until eight-thirty. Mothers carried their babies in shawls wrapped around their shoulders and necks, fathers stood around in circles smoking cigarettes and discussing strategies, and children took advantage of a metal slide that was brought out but never anchored to the ground. In an hour or two it would be too hot for a child to use without getting a second-degree burn.

The man standing next to me nudged me with his elbow and gestured to the slide. "How much money do you think the UNHCR budgeted for this?"

"I'm sure it's a whole amusement park in their reports."

We laughed. He asked if I could spare a smoke, and I pulled out my pack and offered him one. We walked to a spot close to the officer's door, one that by midday would be graced by shade from a nearby building.

"You okay?" He'd noticed the bandages on my leg and scratches on my upper arm.

"Bike accident," I said.

In what felt like a small miracle, my turn was called before the morning turned into afternoon, and I lined up with the others in my range. The officer cursed at people who attempted to sneak into the queue. Two of them—boys with flat-ironed hair who wore makeup and tight pink shirts—received the brunt of his anger.

"It's not your turn yet!" he shouted. "Can you not read? Are you idiots?"

The boys argued between themselves, eyeing the line and the crowd behind us. "It's not safe," they said. "People are giving us dirty looks."

The officer puffed his chest, flared his nostrils, and told them to return to the crowd. Deflated, the boys walked back to an isolated corner holding hands.

"Faggots," the officer muttered.

Inside, the rooms were humid and dirty. A man behind a desk transcribed the basic information from my application into the computer system. He scribbled a long number on the form and sent me to the next door. Another man took my photo before I could pose properly in front of their white screen. I was quickly shuffled to the next stall, where a man asked for my number, pressed my fingers onto an ink pad, and took my prints.

Finally I was told to wait in a large room for a case officer to see me.

The room lacked windows and felt like an oven. A lone fan seemed to only redistribute the hot air. I was soon drenched in sweat. A hallway to my left led to a number of doors. Every few minutes one of them opened and a name was called. A family scurried into the room, then moments later left down the hallway to an unknown destination.

I couldn't tell if it was the heat or the poor ventilation, but my thoughts slowed to a trickle. I closed my eyes, rested my head against the wall, and dreamt of an open sky rolling over a sandy beach. Sunshine warmed my skin, chill beats echoed in my ears, and the smell of fresh flowers filled my nose. A handsome man with well-groomed chest hair and round shoulders offered me a drink: icy, purple, with a little yellow umbrella resting on its rim.

A disembodied voice broke my reverie. "Ramadan? Ahmad Ramadan?"

I jumped out of my seat and walked to the doorway where a woman in a hijab greeted me. Her room was bare: a single office chair behind a desk. No pictures on the walls. A barred window was open, allowing the buzz of refugees in the parking lot to seep in. She closed the door behind me once she realized I wasn't accompanied by a family like the rest of her clients. With no place to sit, I shifted uncomfortably on my feet while she silently examined my papers. She asked me to repeat my basic information and double-checked it on her computer screen.

"Were you involved in the Syrian unrest on either side?" she asked, her eyes never leaving her screen.

"No."

"Are you, or have you ever been, a soldier in the Syrian Arab Army?"

"No."

"Were you involved with the anti-regime groups in any capacity?"

"No."

"Did you participate in any protests, either in support or against the Syrian government?"

"No."

"Did you participate in any criminal activities, such as kidnapping, torturing, smuggling, or any activity that might be considered a war crime?" she deadpanned.

"Would anyone ever say yes to that?" I smirked.

"Just answer the question."

"No. I have not participated in any such criminal activities."

Her questions abruptly paused, as if my comment had made her realize how robotic our exchange had been. She shuffled my papers, typed some more, then rechecked my application.

"Have you ever been arrested by the Syrian regime?" she asked.

I paused. Other than a select few back in Damascus, no one knew of my arrest. A large faction of Lebanese people sympathized with the Syrian regime, so I'd kept the story to myself in Beirut. I was also embarrassed. My prison experience was like a cancerous mole on my face; I just wanted it gone, erased, as if it had never existed.

The case worker glanced up from her screen and looked at me for the first time. I quickly made my decision. "No," I said, "I have never been arrested by the Syrian regime."

She examined me silently, but I stood my ground. Seconds later, the staring contest broke.

"Why did you leave Syria, then?" she asked.

"Because I am gay."

My answer, and possibly my directness, took her aback. She held my gaze for a moment. "You don't look gay." Since arriving in Beirut I had shaved my head, groomed my beard, and gotten into the habit of pumping iron at a cheap gym near my home. The weight training made me feel in control of a body that I'd lost my relationship with. She eyed my black shorts, tight T-shirt, and dirty runners.

"How do gay men look?" I asked.

"Are you just saying this to get resettled in Europe faster?"

I'd heard of such stories: Syrian men escaping their army service and applying to the UNHCR on account of bisexuality or homosexuality in an attempt to get fast-tracked on the resettlement path. Marginalized groups—religious or racial minorities, sexual and gender minorities, single mothers—were desired for resettlement by European countries. And so Syrians quickly learned to game the system: couples got divorced on paper so that the wife and children got priority and the husband could join later; counterfeit documents and fake government IDs were printed to change people's religious affiliations. Although the UNHCR presented reports of organized refugee camps and highly detailed resettlement programming, in reality Lebanon was as chaotic as the Wild West.

When I didn't answer her question, the case worker stared at me for a moment, then shuffled the papers in her hands. "Homosexuality is a sin," she said. "It's one of the biggest sins there is. The throne of Allah up in the sky shakes every single time a man commits this debauchery."

The thought of a throne vibrating to the rhythm of the millions of homosexual acts of penetration committed each day sounded comical to me. I thought to make a joke of the many uses Allah might have for such a quivering chair, but I restrained myself.

"The people of Lot were lifted, then smashed into the ground for their sin," she continued.

"I have been to my fair share of Islamic sermons," I said.

"If we were back in the righteous days of Islam, gay people would be thrown off a high cliff, then rocks would be thrown down upon them."

A couple of years later, the Islamic State of Iraq and Syria would indeed murder gay Syrians by throwing them off the highest buildings and raining stones upon their bodies.

"Am I glad we're not back in those days, then," I said. "Instead we're at the offices of a United Nations division, and I'm assuming you are not speaking on behalf of your employer."

The case worker scoffed. She gathered my papers, checked the numbers one last time, then returned to her screen. I soon heard the printer ticking. She grabbed a single paper printed in colour, signed it, stamped it, and handed it to me. It was divided into two columns, one in English and the other in Arabic. My picture, hazy and barely in focus, crowned the top of the page.

"Keep this registration paper with you at all times," she said. "The UNHCR will call you if you ever will be resettled. Do you have any other questions?"

I carefully folded the paper to put it in my wallet.

"No. They need to see it on your way out." She pointed at the door before returning to her computer screen. I slipped out and walked down the hall toward an empty desk next to the exit, its door held open by a stone. I waited, then popped my head outside to find the guard smoking a cigarette. He absentmindedly examined my paper and told me my application was now complete.

The heat of the day was upon me. I walked on a side road I didn't recognize and followed my unreliable sense of direction until I wound up back at the front entrance to the parking lot. Syrians still gathered; their numbers had multiplied. The metal slide was now abandoned, the air around it wobbly with radiated heat. A woman carried a board covered in cheap sunglasses and attempted to sell them to the masses. A man pushed a small freezer cart around selling bottles of water, pop, and juice. Children laughed and cried. The crowd stretched as far as I could see, countless faces glistening with sweat.

The two boys with their tight shirts and ironed hair stood in a faraway corner, away from the rest. They fearfully watched anyone who might be walking in their direction and exchanged short words in whispers. The guard came out and announced to those waiting that they would have to return tomorrow. As grunts of disappointment and anger filled the air, people swarmed the guard and argued. The gathering grew bigger, and the guard soon retreated inside the building, closing the door. The two boys slipped out a side exit away from the rest. One of them looked back, and our eyes met. I quickly looked the other way.

Then I hurried my step down the familiar road to beat the crowds into public transportation.

◠

I climbed the seven flights of stairs and finally reached the penthouse, winded. Through the door I could hear Michael practising his violin.

Back in the 1950s, this spacious two-floor penthouse must have been the pride and joy of Michael's grandparents, with its massive living room, four bedrooms, and multiple balconies. Its sole bathroom still had wallpaper covered in pink flowers and yellow stars. But in the late seventies, at the start of the Lebanese civil war, it had been abandoned by the family when they immigrated to the United States, never to return. Michael, born and raised in San Francisco, decided to return to his roots in Beirut in the late 2000s. Now the walls were covered with old Lebanese movie posters and vinyl-record sleeves. A massive globe with a secret compartment for liquor bottles sat collecting dust in the second-floor hall next to an old stop sign Michael had carried home one day after seeing it dislodged by a car accident.

I'd rented a room here only days after arriving in Beirut. Just a mattress on the floor, an old leather sofa, and a seventies-style lamp that projected a circle of yellow light onto the wall. Michael, deeply leftist in his views, and aware of his privilege as a white-passing, American-born straight man, went easy on me and charged me below-market rent. He shared his food and weed, asked about my political opinions, and laughed at my jokes, even the silly ones.

"You got the registration?" As he placed his violin back in its case I waved the document in his direction. Then I sat down on the sofa, putting my feet up on the coffee table. A breeze from the balcony brought calm to the room, and we sat in a comfortable silence.

"Are you okay?" he asked.

"I'm not sure." It had dawned on me that I was now a refugee. I understood the term; the concept was simple enough. I'd grown up with the grandchildren of Palestinian refugees in Syria, and I'd witnessed the wave of Iraqi refugees arriving in Damascus following the American invasion in the 2000s. I recalled thinking that it must have been nice: leaving a war-torn country behind, escaping the burning buildings and the intimidating soldiers to sleep safely underneath my country's starry sky. I didn't have to be a contortionist to pat myself on the back for my role in welcoming these refugees. It felt easy, the only logical thing to do. They came from a bad place, and my country was a good place. I was proud—despite the fact that I'd done absolutely nothing.

Now, with a useless piece of paper in my hand, I had morphed into something else: a nightcrawler with no hole to hide in, forced into registration with a massive organization that collected me like a fisherman and placed me in a box with other worms. We watched as their godly hand used us as bait to catch large grants from international bodies. I felt small.

The piece of paper, identifying me as a displaced citizen, didn't offer any stability to my life. If anything, it made the ground under my feet slippery and uncertain. I used to look weeks, months, and years into the future. But as a refugee I had to think only of the present, engaged in a constant fight to make sure I had a land to call my own for the here and now.

My phone buzzed. It was a notification from a local news outlet. I quickly translated it on my screen and forwarded the English version to Liz. A speech by Hassan Nasrallah, the head of the Hezbollah party in Lebanon, was to be televised in less than an hour. As expected, my phone rang.

"I'll need you to live-translate," Liz said. I'd been working with her for two months in a role that had begun as a glorified translator and evolved to include researching, reporting, and interviewing, earning me a couple of bylines in *The Washington Post*. I told Liz I'd do it over Skype, and soon enough I was behind my desk. Then, as the leader of what the West had designated a terrorist organization spoke, I typed an instant translation for Liz to follow.

The bearded man on television, beloved across the Islamic world for taking what he claimed was a stand against the Zionist enemy, spoke of welcoming Syrian refugees in Lebanon and offering them support. He asked his followers to continue to build a good relationship with their Syrian neighbour. At the same time, his troops had reportedly left their stations across the Lebanese–Israeli border to join the war in Syria on the side of the Syrian regime.

I rolled a joint from the stash that lived in my desk drawer and smoked in between the blocks of transcription I was sending. In the first twenty minutes or so, Liz replied to some of these asking for clarification, then slowly she disappeared as well. I was typing into the void, translating a man's lies to an empty hall. Soon Liz texted to let me know that the desk back in D.C. had no interest in the story. She wished me a good night.

"Hey, you sure you're okay?" Michael said from the hallway. "I'm going to Hamra in a bit if you wanna come."

"I have work to do."

Forty-five minutes later I was stoned and the bearded man was still ranting. The night's darkness seeped into my room, but I had no desire to turn on the light. Then the doorbell rang. Friends had unexpectedly arrived to spend the evening: Cee, with a full supply of shish tawook sandwiches; Myriam with her latest girlfriend; and Abdo and his girlfriend, Ro, with Chester, their German shepherd, who ran through the hallway and landed on my bed, tail wagging.

"I texted Cee," Michael said. "I thought you needed the company."

The penthouse, moments ago silent save for the echoes of a moustached leader's speech, now filled with warm greetings, big hugs, and arguments over who ordered the sandwich with no mayo.

The doorbell rang again, and more friends poured in—folks who, like Myriam, had once frequented the Safe Home back in Damascus and then ended up as refugees in Beirut, now each with their own safe home to offer.

Was that the night Cee slept over? Was it the night Chester pushed me off the couch? Did Myriam stay or did she quickly leave with her girlfriend of the week? I don't remember. The memories lose their borders, morph into one. A continuous, endless gathering with friends. Some of these faces filled my home in Beirut for moments, others stayed for months or years. My identity, it occurred to me one of these nights, had never been the documentation I carried or the papers I held in my wallet. It wasn't the officers who told me who I am or the ones who stole parts of me: it had always been the people I belong to. They are my identity card; their love is my constitution.

LOOKALIKE

Here is why he has no place in this narrative.

We walk down to English Bay on the shore of Vancouver months after our breakup. He still looks as handsome as the day I met him in Damascus, though his hair and beard are trimmed shorter. I notice the beaded necklaces and leather wrist straps he now wears— a new habit. It strikes me how foreign yet familiar he feels. He's as jolly and upbeat as he was in the early months of our relationship, when he moved into my rented penthouse with Michael in Beirut. He's far from the sulking man he was in our last months here in Vancouver.

"I met him at his building's gym and sucked him off in the shower," he tells me of his latest hookup. "It was so hot. You should have seen his abs."

He shouldn't have this power over me, but I can't help comparing his vision of this man to my soft belly and wide hips. Maybe if I looked like the Greek statue he sucked off he'd still be in love with me. I smile politely, such a Canadian already.

We arrived together from Lebanon; everyone knew us as a unit. Photographed together, surrounded by our volunteer immigration sponsors. Always seated side by side at dinner tables. Joint Christmas gifts. When we broke up, a collective gasp came from all who knew us in Vancouver.

"I see it all the time with refugee couples," Chris Morrissey told me when she heard the news. As founder of Rainbow Refugee, over the years she'd worked with dozens of queer refugees to bring them to Canada. "Relationships rarely survive the difficulty of the first year."

I nodded but said nothing. In my head I ran through the many fights we had back in Beirut. The times I said I could tell he didn't love me anymore, and that he stayed with me only because I was his ticket to Canada. "You can tell me," I'd said. "We can break up, be friends, arrive together in Canada, then go our separate ways."

"You're insane," he'd said. "Of course I want to be with you."

When we arrive at the logs on the beach, he pulls a baggie from his pocket and expertly rolls a joint. I smirk: I taught him how to roll years ago and smoked his first hash-laced cigarette with him.

"Here." He passes me the smoke, purple fog escaping his nostrils. I shake my head.

"I quit months ago," I say. "It stopped being fun."

He leans with one foot on a log and poses theatrically, his jacket open to the tank top he wears underneath, revealing his armpit. It smelled nice, I recall, when I burrowed my face in there. Before I can help myself I creep closer and our shoulders touch. I regret it instantly.

I made mistakes, of that I am certain. I shouted when I shouldn't have, got angry when I didn't get my way. I am equally to blame for the breakup. I'm not looking to rekindle the relationship, having established how terrible we were to each other. Yet we shared an intimacy—one that sustained us through two years and three months of refugee life in Lebanon—that cannot be replaced. An experience that only the two of us share, that only we will ever understand. He is my twin—scarred by the same deliverance, his trauma an echo of my own. Only he knows what it was really like, what we had to do and what we sacrificed to be able to stand on the sands of English Bay.

Or maybe he understands nothing. Maybe I'm just projecting.

"I actually want to say something." He puffs another cloud. "I want you to know that . . ."

He hesitates. I lean in closer. My ear is inches away from his lips, the way it used to be when we slept next to each other.

"I want you to know that you were right," he says. "I never loved you. I only wanted to come to Canada, and you had a way here."

I jump back as if ambushed by a snake, his body suddenly dangerous to me.

"No, I'm sorry." He steps toward me. "Forget I said anything."

I walk away as quickly as I can on the wet sand. I hear him calling my name. The city stretches ahead of me, its buildings tall and crowded. The road blurs and I almost miss the traffic light telling me to watch for oncoming cars. I hyperventilate. I need to return to my rented one-bedroom apartment. I need the safety of my home. I finally cross the street and run—through the crowd, up streets and alleyways, across my building's lobby, until I'm in the elevator.

I'll be home soon; I will cry about it. Suddenly I could see the dark underside of everything that was good about our relationship. The lovemaking had just been meaningless sex. The laughs we shared a rehearsed con. The support he lent an act. I had ignored my gut and trusted him through it all.

I stare at my reflection in the elevator's mirror: soft belly, wide hips, and tears locked behind tightened eyes. I miss my body, the way it was before him, and I hate that he got to keep his. I hate him. I hate him with all my heart. A burning hate that would agitate volcanos and break the surface of earth. I hate his armpit and his face and the way his eyes twinkle like stars.

But then, can I blame a man faced with the terror of war and promised a land free of homophobia? Would I have done the same thing had I been left with the same options? I might have cheated death for it. I might have fought dragons. I might have lied to a man who genuinely loved me to be able to come here.

Still. I'm human. A man burned by the love of another and burdened by his story. So, he shall be obliterated. He has no place in this story, no weight in this narrative. He won't be mentioned anymore; his influence won't be felt. He will poof away as if he never existed. As if I were a god, with the power to erase him. My refugee twin strangled by our joint umbilical cord. Only I survive on these pages; only my story is delivered.

Some people are just too small to be witnessed.

I sat on the floor next to Liz, who wore a headscarf. A refugee family of eight gathered around us. The mother offered us each a cup of tea, and mine came in a chipped glass.

"Shukran," Liz said. The children giggled at the white woman speaking Arabic.

We were in a room with windows but no windowpanes—just

square holes in the walls covered with plastic sheets. It reminded me of my childhood home. A pile of thin mattresses in one corner, and at the other end kitchen utensils and a small portable propane stove, dirty with coffee stains.

"Tell us what happened," Liz urged in English. I repeated it in Arabic.

"They came last night," the man said, "claiming that the refugees in the makeshift camp harassed one of their women."

The man had tired eyes and bit his nails. As he continued telling the story I whispered it in English to Liz, who took notes. The man elaborated, lost his train of thought, retraced his steps, and struggled to put his story into words. "They set the whole camp on fire. These Christians didn't like that a Muslim refugee camp was built at the outskirts of their village." He became more animated. "The whole camp caught on fire within seconds. All the tents were made of flammable material."

"Where did all the other refugees go?" Liz asked.

"I don't know. We were together there, then each grabbed what they could and ran." He pointed at the walls. "We found this abandoned building last night. But the owner came this morning and asked us to leave."

"What will you do?"

"We will pay him. I don't know with what money, but we will pay him." The man paused, looked at Liz, then looked me straight in the eyes. "Is she rich? Can she pay me?"

I repeated his questions to her, and she shook her head. She explained that it was impossible for her to pay for interviews. "Journalists tell the story, they can't interfere in it," she said. When I translated this the man looked disappointed. He stared at his wife and children, then back at me.

"What about you? What can you do?" he asked.

Earlier that day Liz had called to say that I was to join her on a trip up to the Beqaa Valley in Lebanon's interior. A refugee camp had been set aflame by the locals and she wanted me to help her report on it. As a refugee I wasn't allowed to work in Lebanon, so Liz paid me under the table.

"Be ready in ten," she said over the phone. "I'll pass by with the driver."

An hour into our drive, snow appeared on the road and the driver slowed down. The winter had been harsh that year, with back-to-back snowstorms hitting the valley and its many refugee camps. Snow stayed on the ground until late June. The UNHCR couldn't keep up with the needs of the community, whose many sectarian conflicts proved challenging to navigate.

"The UN can't do shit here," the driver said as we neared the camp. "All they're good at is collecting numbers."

Liz and I exited the car at the broken fences of the burned-down refugee camp. The smell of burned rubber filled my nose. Abandoned objects were scattered across the dark mud: a child's shoe, broken dishes, a ripped jacket, an empty duffle bag bearing a knockoff logo.

"Danny, take photos," Liz instructed.

I pulled out the camera she'd gotten for me and snapped pictures that showed the crimson sunset in the background and the burned tents in the foreground. A close-up of a half-buried radio with a broken antenna. The church beyond the fence.

"Aren't you happy you didn't end up in a refugee camp?" Liz joked on the way home, breaking the silence in the car. Beirut appeared after we took a final descent from the mountains: glittery, loud, full of possibilities.

On weekends we'd pile into a car and drive up and down the short Lebanese coast.

Such a tiny country—you could drive it from its Syrian border to its Israeli one in two hours. We made our way to the public beach we always ended up on: a small piece of rocky land sandwiched between two hotels. Most of the Lebanese shore was privately owned and operated and accessed only by paying a hefty fee. We grabbed our coolers and folding chairs and walked across the sharp rocks to our spot.

We were three Syrians and one Lebanese, the same four every day: Abdo, a fellow refugee who'd brought his dog with him from Aleppo and vowed not to cut his hair until he was back in his hometown; Ro, Abdo's girlfriend, a bisexual woman whose laughter was louder than the crashing waves of the Mediterranean, and whom I'd gotten to know when she visited the Safe Home back in Damascus; Cee, the sweetest introvert you'd ever meet, who'd picked me up at the border when I first arrived in Lebanon and helped me find my apartment, gifted me with shoes, and financed a replacement for my laptop that remained somewhere in the Damascus International Airport; and finally, myself, the appointed cynic of the group.

We spent most of the day drinking on the beach, playfully pushing one another in the water, and suntanning on the rocks. We'd read somewhere that beaches like this one were still public because in Lebanon that's where the sewer system emptied into the sea. We had no other option, though—not when the cheapest private beach charged forty U.S. dollars to enter. So we kept going back.

By sunset, we were drunk. We gathered our things and returned to the car.

"Where to now?" Abdo asked. He'd had lots to drink, so his driving was wobbly at best.

I shrugged. Someone pulled out pre-rolled hash cigarettes and lit one. We rolled up our windows and hotboxed the car with the smoke while we drove crowded highways with no lane markings. Abdo headed toward Beirut's Gemmayzeh neighbourhood.

"Fuck, it's a checkpoint," he said. "Roll down your windows."

We slid up to the Lebanese Army checkpoint, smoke oozing out the vehicle. I held my breath, as I tended to laugh at the smallest, silliest things when I was high. The sun-kissed soldier asked for all our papers. I pulled my Syrian passport out of a backpack and handed it to him.

The soldier was in his early twenties. Syrians make fun of Lebanese soldiers—a leftover pastime from the Syrian occupation of Lebanon between 1976 and 2005. In my childhood I'd heard jokes about how Lebanese soldiers were never man enough to stand up to the Syrians, how they were all faggots. The soldier holding my passport had well-manicured nails. When I handed it to him I'd felt his soft skin. Was he part of our queer family? Maybe this whole thing could go away if I promised him a date?

The passport—cracked and worn from months of being carried around in my back pocket—bent in the soldier's hands. He compared my aging face to my teenage picture, then asked me to point out the page with the Lebanese visa.

I flipped past the twenty pages covered in stamps for him.

"You're a refugee?" he asked.

"My visa says I am a tourist." Whoever was sitting next to me squeezed my thigh as a warning.

"What are you doing here, then?" he said.

"Touring . . ."

Chuckles from my fellow passengers were quickly hushed. The soldier held my passport between his hands as if he was about to tear it apart. "Are you being a smartass?"

"No, sir. Sorry, sir. Yes, I'm a refugee." I pulled my UNHCR paper out, but he ignored it. "I came here a couple months ago."

"Are you all refugees?" he asked. Three of us nodded. "And you own a car? Five-star refugees. Do you park it outside your tent?"

Silence fell upon us. The soldier, amused by his own joke, laughed, the M16 rifle resting against his shoulder bobbing up and down.

"Are we free to go now, sir?" Abdo's voice was calm.

"The hell you are," the soldier said. He walked away to show my passport to his supervisor.

"Did you have to be such a bitch, Danny?" Ro asked. Her tone was, as always, somewhere between frustration and amusement.

"What do you want me to say?" I asked, then switched to a heavy Syrian accent. "Yes, sir. I am a dumb refugee. Please don't shoot me. They burned my house. They killed my mother-in-law."

"No, but maybe try not to get us all arrested?"

"Their government doesn't want to give me refugee status, and I'm left with a tourist visa. We all are. So why would I call myself a refugee if they won't even admit that I am one?"

"Come down from the soapbox, Danny," Abdo said.

"It's stupid. This whole thing is stupid." I was getting louder now. The soldiers looked back at us. "It's complicated and it makes no sense. I don't know what I am anymore. Do you?"

"Okay, calm down, kids," Cee said. He pulled his door handle and stepped out of the car. We silently watched him walk toward the soldiers. We heard snippets as he spoke to them with his Lebanese accent, then opened his wallet and showed them his ID. In his wallet, twenties and fifties appeared. He theatrically pulled out fifty U.S. dollars and kept it in his hand while he returned his wallet to his pocket. Then he shook the guard's hand, leaving the money there. The guard smiled and handed the passports back. With steady steps, Cee returned to the car. Proud of himself, he smiled as he threw the passport back at me. The soldier waved us through, and we drove in silence all the way to my apartment.

◖

My task for the day was to find out how many people had really been killed in a massacre committed by the Assad army in a small town on the outskirts of Aleppo. The number mattered: If it did not exceed the total sum of victims in the last massacre, would it be worth reporting?

I rang my usual contacts in the Free Syrian Army, as well as the on-ground local reporters, and asked for numbers. The reports were conflicting, even emotional. Hundreds, one person claimed. Mothers and children had been targeted, another insisted.

"Your newspaper is on the desk of Obama every morning," a contact noted, lecturing me on the inaction of the West. "Why don't you report the truth?"

"How many were murdered in the massacre?" I asked again.

"This blood is on these so-called world leaders' hands," he continued.

"But how many do you know were murdered?"

"They were all killed with white weapons," he said, referring to knives and swords as opposed to black weapons like bullets or poison gas. "What a tragedy."

"I need to know how many were killed."

"I don't know. I'm in Turkey," he finally admitted. "I fled Syria a week ago."

Giving up on contacts, I moved to my next tried-and-true method. I bookmarked all the YouTube videos posted by the rebels on the ground after the massacre. They'd walked around with their handheld devices, smartphones, and GoPro cameras recording footage of the bodies gathered in a school backyard, all the while reciting lines from the Quran by heart and cursing Assad, Obama, and both Britain and France for not doing enough to save the people. On a piece of paper, I started counting.

1. Brown hair. Blood on face. Mouth open.
2. Child. Maybe twelve. Blue T-shirt.
3. Man. His head is smashed in. Nose broken. Crooked teeth.

I watched one video after another, making sure not to count the same victim twice. I drew a little map of the backyard, marking an X and a number where each body had been left to rot. In the videos, I followed the path of each rebel and saw glimpses of the other rebels filming. I pinpointed each path.

22. An older man. Maybe in his sixties. Headscarf. Wound in his neck.
23. A man in his twenties. Strawberry blond beard. Dark brown hair. A birthmark on his right cheek.

I paused. It took me a second to realize why that last face stood out. I rewound the video. This man looked just like me. A distant cousin, perhaps, or a trick of the eye. I couldn't tell. Suddenly I couldn't breathe. My toes and fingers went numb, my vision blurred, and my apartment felt cold despite the fact that it was mid-August.

I wondered if he'd died instantly. If a stroke of darkness had come upon him, then left him untethered to this earth, floating away from a pool of blood and body parts. Had he prolonged his own foretold death? His soul skinned away from him throughout the cold desert night. Ticking away like a broken clock. Slipping unwitnessed except by other glassy eyes. I wondered if his neck had been kissed before it was slit. If his birthmark had been smiled upon before being drenched with his own blood. I wondered if he'd cried in his last moments. If he'd called for his mother. If he'd remembered his sisters. If he'd wanted to stay.

I sprang out of my seat and dug into my backpack for my hash. I rolled myself a joint with too much hash and not enough tobacco. I pulled a breath in, the purple smoke burning my throat. I coughed until tears rolled down my cheeks, then pulled another inhale. I relaxed on my mattress on the floor and slowly got lost in the haze.

Two hours later, my phone rang.

"Hey, did you get the numbers?" Liz asked.

"Yeah." I cleared my throat. "Twenty-three."

"Why didn't you text me?"

"It took a lot of time to do it. I had to count them myself."

"Okay," she said. "Twenty-three."

"Yeah."

"I'll have to get back to you if we need a story. I need to ask the newsroom before they close for the night."

"Sure."

I didn't hear back from her that day.

A powerful car bomb flung glass and heavy strips of metal across a wide intersection in downtown Beirut on Friday, killing a former cabinet minister and underscoring Lebanon's growing instability as it absorbs the impact of neighboring Syria's increasingly bloody civil war.

THE WASHINGTON POST, DECEMBER 27, 2013

My windows shook. A frame gave in and a sheet of glass slipped off and slammed to the floor, smashing into pieces. It was eight in the morning and I was nursing a hangover from the night before. As I stared at the broken glass in a daze, I heard a loud boom.

"Fuck," I muttered.

My phone rang. Not Liz, who was in London, but another journalist who was in town, and she needed an update. "Can you come right now?" she asked.

"Come where?"

"To the explosion site."

"Why?"

She sighed, frustrated. I admit that back then I was quite disillusioned with journalism. I didn't have that hunger white journalists had for a good story: an explosion that rocks a city's downtown core; an extremist group amputating someone's hand live on Twitter; an all-female rebel militia. I would read the articles we produced and see the ways in which they'd been framed to evoke emotion from Western readers. They always told the truth, mind you. They were just very strategic about what verbs to use, whose quote to feature. They never inserted their opinions, but their allegiance showed between the lines. I was also jaded: one too many broken faces on my screen, one too many children crying. One too many leaders with bullshit speeches to be translated and transcribed so that a white boomer in Wisconsin could shake his head and call us savages.

"I'm at the Hariri statue. Be here in ten minutes." The journalist hung up.

I got out of bed and knocked on the door of my shared bathroom to make sure Michael wasn't using it. I stood in the shower and prayed for running water. A drizzle trickled out of the shower head. It smelled like the sea. I quickly scrubbed my body and hair, then used the last bit of water to wash the soap away. No time to shave. I dried off, put on yesterday's underwear and a pair of jeans, and ran out the door with my camera on my shoulder and a pastry in my mouth.

I had to hurry. No taxis would take me to the explosion site, and everyone was running away from it. I pushed my way through the crowd, leading with my shoulder and ducking to avoid elbows. Finally I saw the journalist standing by herself under the statue of Rafic Hariri, the slain prime minister.

"Where were you?" she asked. "We'll be late!"

"We are late. The explosion has already happened."

She gave me a dirty look and started walking. I followed her, snapping photos of everything we passed. An ambulance rushed out, its back doors open, allowing a glimpse of three covered bodies surrounded by sombre-looking passengers. It stopped at an inter-section and lazily let people cross.

"Ask them how many people died," the journalist whispered to me.

"Hey, how many are dead?" I shouted to the passengers in Arabic. No one answered. I repeated my question, and one of them looked at me. "Do you know? How many dead?" I asked again. The man silently gazed at me with a face carved in wood, sitting on the side chair, hands in his lap. As the ambulance drove off, his eyes remained locked on mine.

"Why won't they respond?" the journalist asked.

We walked closer to the explosion site, passing abandoned build-ings covered in graffiti and bullet holes from the previous civil war, then newer ones with shattered windows, the glass in piles below them on the street. The hubbub died down until the only sound we heard was the dragging of the metal barriers military personnel were erecting around the site. Road dividers—big boulders of cement that took machines to install—had been pushed aside by the explosion. A water feature at the entrance of a modern building continued to run, but cracks in the pool's edges allowed it to pour out everywhere. It snaked through the debris, carrying with it streaks of blood. The December sun cared nothing for the mess and filled the sky with a fuzzy warmth, as if inviting people to come outside and witness the destruction.

"Ask him to let us in." The journalist pointed out a guard at one of the hastily set up barriers. "Tell him we're journalists."

I argued with the guard in Arabic, then turned and told her he wouldn't allow it.

"Why?" she said, almost angry, as if she were entitled to the story.

"Because it's an explosion site."

She stopped, looked me straight in the eye, and told me to watch myself. "You're letting your emotions lead you, Danny," she said. "That's not how journalism works. That's not how you get ahead in this game. You need to divorce your emotions or else you'll be a fixer for the rest of your life, and never a journalist."

"That's easy for you to say," I snapped back, "when the people dying don't look like you or speak your language."

"You're in a better position than I am," she said. "You could be the next . . ."

I assumed she was searching her memory for the name of a single famed Syrian journalist. The pause grew and became more awkward. "It doesn't matter," she said firmly. "Just try to work with me here."

"What do you want me to do?"

She looked around, confused, then walked toward a group of army officers huddled together; I followed her.

I knew I did not want to be a journalist anymore.

DEPARTURE (2)

It was past midnight on a Saturday in September but still hot in Beirut.

Cee and I took a corner at the rooftop bar, away from the dancers. The loudspeakers behind us echoed across the open skies as the Mediterranean stretched ahead, dark like the inside of a fist. We turned our backs to our friends and gazed out silently, nursing our fruity drinks, holding them over the edge between our palms. The sea breeze seeped into our clothes: Cee had lent me a fancy shirt so that the bouncer would let me in.

"Excited?" Cee asked.

"I guess."

This wasn't the first piece of clothing Cee had passed down to me. Upon my arrival in Beirut, over two years before, he'd brought me a suitcase full of T-shirts, shorts, and fancy shoes. I'd first met him on one of my earlier trips to Beirut, and we'd become friends in the way many queer men do, by going on a doomed first date. He was heartbroken after a difficult breakup, seriously attempting to gauge our potential for a future together. I was a party boy unable to commit to a plant, let alone a human. A tale as old as time.

I cozied up to my best friend, and he put his arm around me. We stood, leaning a bit over the edge, quiet for some time. Then the music changed.

"I love this song," he announced. He ran back and broke into our circle of dancing friends. After listening for a couple of seconds, counting the belly-dancing steps in his head, he began engaging his hips and twirling his thighs. He rested a finger on his forehead then rolled his lower back, exaggerating his hip loop. He caught my eye and we exchanged a smile.

I was packed. Luggage full of summer clothing that I'd never wear again in the cold of Canada and shoes with holes that I'd replace with boots soon enough. My flight to Vancouver was booked. Over twenty-six hours of airports, layovers, and paperwork were ahead of me. Tonight, however, we danced. Someone dragged me into the heart of the circle and I belly danced with Cee. The close friends who'd gathered to bid me farewell formed a ring around us and clapped. Cee and I imitated each other, coordinating our hip thrusts to the beat. A friend climbed onto a table and belly danced atop it. Laughter and applause took over. Cee, self-conscious, escaped back to our quiet spot. I followed him.

The waiter had taken our abandoned drinks, and we both sighed in frustration. Below us the corniche extended into the distance under dimmed streetlights: families on picnic blankets with hot tea and argilehs, teenagers shouting at one another, couples holding hands. Syrian children sold balloons, chewing gum, and single red roses wrapped in plastic to lovers walking the seashore. If you didn't buy from them they'd beg for money anyway.

"I'm going to miss you," Cee said.

"I dare you to join me, then," I replied with a smile.

I didn't know it yet, but he would take the dare seriously. While I found my way to Canada as a privately sponsored refugee, he would apply as a skilled worker and arrive in Canada less than a year after me. He'll mention this night in his best man speech at my wedding seven years later.

By four in the morning our group was wobbling around drunk. The rooftop club was still open, but we needed to leave before we made fools of ourselves. We crowded the elevator down and leaned on one another as we jaywalked across the highway. McDonald's, stationed like a coast guard office right on the water, collected us. We sat silently munching on burgers and salted fries, the music of the club still stuck in our ears. Some said their goodbyes while others stayed with nowhere else to go. The remaining friends walked to my apartment and climbed the stairs, shushing one another so as not to wake the neighbours. Doors creaked and floors ached under our feet.

I took off Cee's fancy shirt, now drenched with sweat, and sat behind my desk to roll a joint. The remaining four created a cuddle puddle on the mattress. I lit up and passed the joint around. Cee shook his head.

"More for us," I said.

The sunrise light came peeking through the plastic sheet covering my broken window. I opened it and leaned out. Then, without a second thought, I sat on the windowsill and slid my legs outside.

"Are you insane?" Cee shouted.

"Come and look."

From behind he wrapped his arms around my waist to anchor me. I felt his chin on my shoulder as I pointed out the glimmer of sun in the distance. The others joined me on the ledge, legs dangling, nothing between us and the ground seven floors below. We watched the sunrise glow.

"I'm going to miss you, you silly thing," I whispered to Cee.

The Private Sponsorship of Refugees, a program unique to Canada, allows its citizens and permanent residents to support the resettlement of refugees in the country. In essence, it's meant to offer a way for Canadians to engage with the global refugee crisis in a meaningful, proactive way.

To put it simply, five to seven Canadians form a sponsorship circle and then somehow find a refugee they want to sponsor. They apply to the federal government with their intention, find a nonprofit organization—also known as a Sponsorship Agreement Holder (SAH)—to manage their sponsorship, and raise enough money to support the refugee financially in their first year in Canada.

The federal government then triggers a process in which its embassy approaches the refugee, offers them settlement, and whisks them away to Canada. When they arrive, the newcomer sheds their refugee status and becomes a permanent resident. Three years later, this former refugee is allowed to apply for Canadian citizenship.

Sounds easy, right? Well, not so much. The process is tediously long, with bureaucratic delays at every step: it takes months to raise the amount of money required to sponsor one refugee, then months for the application to be processed through the SAHs and the federal government before it's sent to a Canadian embassy, which then takes months to approach the refugee and help the resettlement.

In my case, the process took a bit under two years. And at the time of writing this book, in certain embassies the wait might be up to seven years.

Refugee sponsorship circles, run by volunteers, rarely make their full term. Many folks with good intentions realize, late in the game, that refugee sponsorship is a lot of work. It's dealing with the rebuilding of someone's life from scratch in a new and foreign land over the span of multiple years. The commitment becomes daunting, and the circle falls in on itself.

Back when I was privately sponsored, any person could volunteer to be part of a circle. No interview or background checks were required. This opened the door to clashes between refugees and their sponsors, who might have taken on the role to fulfil a personal need rather than to support a fellow human. I hear that a police check and signature on a sponsorship agreement are now required; this is a good first step.

But to this day, no cultural training is offered to either the sponsors or the refugees. No one teaches the sponsors about the nuanced needs of a refugee based on their culture, racial identity, gender identity, sexual orientation, religious background, or personal history of trauma. And no one offers the refugees a crash course in Canadian history: neither the bright pages of achievements nor the bloody pages of colonization. There's no clear training on how to file your taxes, plan your career, recredit your university degree, or find meaningful communities.

In my case, I was approached by a Syrian Canadian man who followed me on Twitter and introduced me to Rainbow Refugee. This SAH organization, based in Vancouver, promised to put together a sponsorship circle for me—and months later, seven gay men in Canada, most of them a generation above me, had joined it. The Syrian Canadian, Ghassan, kept me in the loop for months as the circle was being assembled. We mainly talked about ourselves, flirted some, and compared our Syrian estrangements.

"I found a treasure this morning, and I want your help with the Arabic," he wrote me once on Facebook Messenger. "I forgot that I had hours of voice memos on my phone from two and a half years ago when I was coming out to my mother. I was enduring the worst from my parents during that BS. I recorded all of it."

"Wow!" I texted back, knee-deep in an article I was researching for Liz.

"There's this one memo where my mother is reading me a poem in Arabic. It's a poem she wrote about my coming out. It's honestly harsh."

I paused what I was doing and looked at the screen. Ghassan, whom I'd never met in real life, had gotten comfortable sharing his stories with me. It gave him a sense of peace, perhaps, to find someone like him—out of the closet and struggling to stay on good terms with his parents.

"When we Skype next, you've got to hear it. I need your help translating," he wrote.

It was the first time I felt that I might have some wisdom to share, a dear friend who was going through what I went through. I didn't know what I would tell him, but I knew I could offer him empathy at the very least.

But Ghassan was soon replaced by another sponsor without any explanation.

Meanwhile, before the circle could apply for my immigration application, they needed to raise the money to accompany it.

"Danny, we wanted to talk to you about something," one of my sponsors, a man with a moustache and an air of self-importance, said to me over Skype. "We've discussed it, and we need you to stop posting photos on Facebook."

The previous weekend I'd gone with Cee and others to a beach-front hotel with a pool, using a discount coupon we'd found online. We smuggled in cheap beer and coolers and spent the afternoon swimming and suntanning. That evening, when I got home, I posted a couple of photos on Facebook.

"You see, it's hard to raise money for you when people here can see your profile," the man said. "When you post happy photos on private beaches, people might not be inclined to donate to your cause."

"You're fundraising for me became I'm gay, not because I'm poor," I countered.

"If you're happy in Beirut, why would people want to bring you to Canada?"

Turns out I wasn't allowed to be happy while I waited for my immigration. Should I have been in a constant state of terror, waiting for my saviours? Maybe a video of me sitting meekly on the dirty ground of a refugee camp, face covered in tar, eyes sparkly with tears, would be better for the fundraising goals.

"Just don't do it, Danny," he said firmly. "It's for your own good."

After that conversation I changed my Facebook privacy settings to limit my posts to local friends. Privately I emailed Chris at Rainbow Refugee and asked if I could get a different liaison for the sponsorship group.

Over the next months I was informed of various fundraising efforts. I witnessed social media videos and photos of events where my white sponsors wore traditional Saudi outfits they'd mistaken for Syrian and watched a white "belly dancer" swerve her hips uncontrollably. They projected my picture onto the wall and asked people to donate to my cause. It all felt wrong to me, as if I were being paraded across Vancouver, asking for handouts.

Finally Chris confirmed that my sponsors had passed the funding threshold and could now submit my application to the federal government. Documents were sent my way and I spent days filling them out. On more than a hundred and fifty pages were questions about all sorts of things, many of them repeated in different shapes and forms, as if to trip me up into revealing a lie.

Once I was done, it became a waiting game. The government needed time to process the application, and I had nothing to do but anticipate their call. I took my phone with me to the shower; I kept it on at night. I checked the immigration ministry's website on a daily basis for updates. The idea of leaving the Middle East and arriving in a gay-friendly world felt pressing—as if I'd been in hibernation and that my spring was upon me. I rarely spoke of anything else to friends. The idea grew bigger and more encompassing. With every setback in Beirut I reminded myself that I'd be leaving soon, never to return. I smoked joints and watched YouTube videos of Vancouver, its Pride parade, its many neighbourhoods and the people who lived in them. I ran on autopilot, almost unaware of the magnitude of the step I was taking.

"Go. Leave this town that never liked you behind," Cee said when I gave him an update at an ice cream shop. "Take me with you if you can."

We laughed. The woman behind the counter handed me my cone and we sat on pink chairs that looked as though they'd been stolen from Willy Wonka's factory.

"The sponsors are driving me nuts," I told him, mouth full of soft serve. "There's a lot of infighting, and they keep replacing members. I don't know what's happening over there."

"You're not married to them," he said bluntly. "When you get there, say thank you and move on."

I waited. The waiting was interrupted by trips to refugee camps, counting bodies in YouTube videos, and explosions in the early hours of the morning. It was soothed by bar-hopping nights, underground drag performances, and enough vodka to light up a distillery. By the hugs I exchanged with friends, the kisses I stole in forbidden places, the hunger I felt for more—more joy, more happiness, deeper feelings, harder kisses, more books to sign, more art to create. Days bled into one another, and my internal clock went haywire. The hashish tangled in my brain and made me hazy; my world fogged up with it. Life was a beautiful painting and I'd dropped a bucket of water on it, blurring the colours.

"Are you okay, Danny?" Gary, one of my sponsors, texted me on Facebook.

"I don't think I am," I replied.

Gary told me he'd grown up in a family that favoured his older brother. His parents made him feel inferior and belittled, and they weren't comfortable with his sexuality. He couldn't wait to leave the family home; he'd never made peace with his upbringing.

He'd travelled the world and loved to recount tales of his adventures. Like the time he saw Christopher Reeve in a gym locker room in New York and got a full-frontal view of Superman. Or the time he made the last train from London to Paris, falling asleep with a view of the Thames and waking to sunrise over the Seine. Or the day he bought his apartment in Vancouver and filled it with mementos from his many journeys.

"That privileged prick," he'd said when I relayed my conversation with the moustached man. "He's only doing this to gain favour in the community."

"Not like you," I said.

"Not like me," he insisted.

I grew fond of Gary. We connected over stories of our similar upbringings. He helped me fill out my immigration application, paid for my dog's vet bills, and spent hours texting with me every day. My other sponsors were challenging to talk to. They spoke to me the way I spoke to my dog when he didn't follow my commands: in firm, short, and patronizingly easy-to-understand sentences. Gary, on the other hand, treated me as an actual living, breathing human being. That, unsurprisingly, felt nice.

Gary wanted to hear my stories. Although I bristled at the idea of sharing my traumatic history with most people, I was comfortable doing so with Gary. He nodded as I talked, smiled when I made jokes, and teared up when I did. I told him about my abusive parents, my career woes in Egypt, the Safe Home in Damascus. One thing I kept close to my chest was my arrest, which I still wanted to erase from my memory.

"You're in love with this man," Cee had told me over ice cream that day. "You talk to him every day, you text him all the time, he's flying here just to see you. You're totally in love."

"Shut up," I said, louder than anticipated. "I am not in love with Gary."

I didn't want to be with him, I wanted to *be* him: the successful career, the stable job, the established home in Vancouver, the leisure time for going to the gym, the fancy clothes he wore. Immigration to Canada stopped being an abstract concept and became an achievable goal. I now had a model to look to, and that model was Gary.

"When you arrive, we'll find you a job at a local newspaper," he said over Skype. "Something light and fun, like reporting on community events or concerts. No more war-zone reporting for you."

"When you arrive, we'll find you an apartment with everything you need," he texted on WhatsApp. "A big bed, a nice hot shower, a backyard for the dog to play in."

"When you arrive, we'll go out to Davie Street and party with the best of them," he messaged on Facebook. "We'll be snazzy and fun."

Yes. A million yeses. Hash smoke filled my head with images of returning to my lovely apartment, tape recorder in my pocket, happy dog awaiting me. Watching the Pride parade videos, I melted into the screen and became one of the marchers. Rainbow crown on my head, megaphone in my hand. I wanted it. I wanted it all. And Gary was offering it to me on a silver platter.

He became the only person I spoke to from Canada, my only contact with what was happening on the ground there. He was jaded about the support others seemingly rarely offered.

For his birthday that year, Gary got on an airplane and came to visit me in Beirut. He'd booked a fancy hotel nearby but insisted on staying at my place one evening after coming down with a cold. He slept in my bed that night, cuddling up next to me.

I woke up at two a.m. and kept silent as he felt my chest and upper body with both hands.

In June of 2014 I received a phone call from Beirut's Canadian embassy inviting me in for an immigration interview. That call had been expected in March, and for the past four months I'd never had my phone on silent. I continued to take it with me to the bathroom and the shower and left it to vibrate under my pillow at night.

The interview, which lasted a total of eight minutes, concluded with a simple note: I was scheduled to move to Canada in three months.

Outside the Canadian embassy, I called Gary and told him the good news. I giggled in ecstasy, tears welling in my eyes.

"We've got to find you an apartment as soon as possible," he said. "I have to do all the work. No one in the circle cares about this as much as I do."

Over the past few months I'd heard lots from Gary about the other sponsors getting bored with the wait and losing interest in supporting the application. Slowly, Gary had replaced most of my original circle of support with personal friends of his.

"These boys are busy partying it up on Davie," Gary said.

"Thank you for all you do," I said. "I'm very grateful."

"Are you going to post about this on Facebook?" he asked.

"Yes, of course."

"Don't forget to tag me in the post."

⌒

My final meeting with Liz Sly was much easier than I'd expected. Our agreement to end things seemed to be quite mutual, to the point that I felt uneasy about how comfortable she was letting me go.

"I think it's time for us to find some fresh blood," she said, sitting in the café downstairs from her apartment on Hamra Street in the heart of Beirut. I nodded.

"Would you write me a recommendation letter?" I asked.

Liz said she would. "You know," she added, "you'll face a lot of challenges finding a job in journalism in North America. Most local articles are written by fresh-out-of-college students for cheap. That's why a lot of young journalists travel to remote places like the Middle East and Far Asia to have an opportunity."

"Oh?" I said, uninterested. I was planning on getting whatever job I could find. By then I was already writing articles for a Canadian LGBTQ+ magazine, reporting on queer communities in the Middle East.

She asked me what I was hoping to do in Canada, and I told her that I'd been writing a novel.

"While on the job?" she joked.

I laughed awkwardly. Yes, probably while on the job.

"What's it about?"

"It's called *The Clothesline Swing*. I've been working on it for years." In truth, every time I got stoned I felt so jittery and broken that I had to write. I hadn't planned to write a novel, but I just kept returning to the same Word document and fishing a story out. By then the word count had reached almost two hundred thousand. In its rough state it was so confusing that I highly doubted anyone but me would be able to decipher it.

I recounted the plot to Liz, and she listened absentmindedly. When she finally started scrolling her phone, I trailed off.

"Well, good luck," she said, paying for our coffees. "You're going to need it."

On a warm night that September, Cee picked me up at my apartment. I said goodbye to Michael and trudged down the long flight of stairs for the last time. My plane ticket had been upgraded to business class: Gary's doing, all the way from Canada.

"Fancy." Cee whistled. "That man wants to sleep with you."

"Give it up already," I joked, sliding into the passenger seat.

On the way to the airport we were stopped at a military checkpoint. The officer asked for my passport and flipped through to the Canadian visa page.

"What's this?" he asked. I explained that I was immigrating to Canada.

"You lucky son of a bitch," he said. I worried that he might tear the passport apart. "You fucking Syrians leave for Europe and America and leave us Lebanese behind."

"I'm sorry," I said. I didn't know why I apologized.

"Go. Never come back, you hear?" He tossed the passport through the window at my face. "This place doesn't want you. We don't want you here."

I sighed and rolled up my window. For the last moments of our trip Cee and I remained silent, the heaviness of goodbye on our shoulders. Finally the lights of the airport appeared in the distance.

"Never come back," Cee said quietly. "This place doesn't want you here."

I nodded, collected my Syrian passport to use for the last time, and dragged my luggage up the ramp and across the pavement. Then the automatic glass doors opened and the noise of the airport swallowed me away.

HUGS

When I arrived in Canada, Gary had already rented me an apartment in a residential neighbourhood called Marpole in south Vancouver. The ground-floor apartment had no privacy until I closed the curtains, and no sunlight unless I opened them. It was a ten-minute drive from Gary's but otherwise far away from any grocery stores, transit, or nightlife. He'd paid for furniture and appliances out of his own pocket: a bed from Ikea, a leather sofa inspired by my penchant for leather jackets, a toaster, a blender. He'd accepted donations from his friends: a comfortable red loveseat, a secondhand television set. He dedicated his days to me, showing up as early as nine in the morning and staying until bedtime.

"Thank you so much for all you do," I said a week in. "But maybe I'll take the day tomorrow to rest and unpack."

"Don't worry," he said, smiling. "I'll come and help you unpack. I don't have much going on tomorrow."

I nodded politely.

Gary had a lot to say about everyone else in the community. If I chatted someone up, he'd tell me of the many negative experiences he'd had with them personally or heard about through the grapevine.

If another of my sponsors wanted to hang out, he'd demand to be included, then dominate the conversation.

"Self-serving cowards," Gary said when sponsors began dropping from the circle like flies. "They didn't have what it takes."

He hugged me and told me not to worry and that everything would be all right. "I'll take care of you," he said.

Mitch, the only other sponsor who remained in my circle, kept in touch from afar. One day he asked if he could come over to drop off a gift, which turned out to be a painting of an angel dressed in Roman garb.

"It's by a dear friend of mine," he said, presenting the large canvas. "Made me think of you."

Wary of another man trying to get into my life, I politely declined the gift. Mitch did not hide his disappointment. "Don't you like it?" he asked.

"I don't think it would fit with the decor Gary made for this home," I said.

Mitch nodded and accepted the painting back.

"Mitch is a snake, and you need to be careful," Gary told me later. "He talked shit about you all over town."

When Ghassan, the Syrian Canadian who had originally helmed my sponsorship circle, wanted to take me out for dinner, Gary invited himself along. I made it clear that I just wanted to spend some time with a fellow Syrian.

"We'll be speaking Arabic," I texted him. "You won't understand a word."

"Then speak in English," he texted back. "You can't do me this simple favour after all I did for you?"

I ignored him, put my phone on silent, and slid it into my back pocket. Ghassan drove to Marpole, and we finally met in person. We hugged and kissed each other on the cheek. "Ahleen," he said, and I smiled. He drove us to Davie Village, and we ended up spending the evening talking in the Fountainhead Pub. The streets were busy with folks he knew, or folks we wanted to get to know. Puddles of rain reflected the neon signs of bars like Junction and Numbers.

"I can't believe you've been here a month and you haven't been to Davie Village yet," Ghassan said, waving hello to another person passing by.

"Well, I was busy."

"With Gary, I assume," he said.

"He can be overbearing," I said, choosing my words carefully. "But the guy is spending so much money and taking so much of his time to ensure I have everything I need."

Ghassan took my hand. "Danny, we didn't want to bring this up to you while you were in Beirut, but Gary is a challenging man."

"How so?" I felt I already knew the answer.

"He can become obsessive," he said. "He made the circle quite toxic, and that's why we all dropped out. He had to find other people to fill out our spots."

"I agree that he can be difficult, but I think it comes from a good place," I said. "He seems genuinely interested in helping."

Ghassan shrugged. We got up from our spot in the café and went to stand in the line for Junction. Ghassan asked if this was my first time going to a gay bar.

"No, there are a couple in Beirut, one in Istanbul, in Kuala Lumpur."

"Beirut, you say?" Ghassan smiled. "Wow. Never thought I'd hear of such a thing."

He dropped me off at my apartment around two in the morning. At the door, while taking my shoes off, I finally checked my phone. Eight missed calls, and over thirty messages from Gary. I sighed and scrolled through them. What started as short I-hope-you're-having-a-good-evening sentiments quickly evolved into long paragraphs with capitalized words and multiple exclamation points. Gary accused Ghassan of reaping the fruits of his labour and claimed that everyone in Vancouver except him was befriending me only to gain status and to feel good about their charitable selves. "You are my refugee," he wrote. "I worked hard to get you here. Why would you repay me with such cruelty? Why won't you respond to my texts?"

I threw the phone across the bed. Then it rang.

"Hey," I said. "I just got home."

"Why would you ignore me for this long?" It sounded as though he was crying. "I thought you cared for me."

"Gary, of course I care for you. I just need some time on my own. I needed to see my friend and go out for an evening."

"You could have said so. I can take you out. There's this new bar that just opened, a fancy place with good company. Not the grungy Village."

"You don't understand," I said. "I just arrived here, Gary, and I need to make friends and get to know the city. I don't even know how to get around town yet."

"I can teach you. It's my responsibility as your sponsor to teach you," he insisted. "Why won't you let me help you?"

"You're not listening. I need some time alone. I cannot be preoccupied with you all the time."

"Is this how you repay me?" he said. "You're being an ungrateful bitch."

I hung up on him, turned off my phone, and took my clothes off. I shivered in the cool air of the bedroom, then slipped into bed. I opened my bedside drawer and lit a joint, having already disabled the smoke detector.

Half an hour later Gary was knocking on my door, demanding to talk it through "like adults."

I stood naked on the other side of the door and asked him to go home. "Please, let's talk about this in the morning." There was a pressure growing in my chest, right around my broken rib. It felt as if I'd swallowed a hot stone that was now stuck in my windpipe. Gary knocked again. I put on pants and opened the door shirtless.

"Can we talk about this tomorrow?" I repeated, but he pushed past me. For the next hour we talked in circles, and no matter what I tried he always had a way to direct the conversation back into a place of hurt.

Finally, as the morning light seeped into the living room, I learned how to calm Gary down and get him off my back.

"I'm so sorry, honey," I whispered, faking a smile and cozying up next to him. "You're absolutely right, I should never have gone out without you."

He seemed to deflate and settle like a punctured balloon.

"You were correct," I continued, craving my bed, "they're all horrible people. I'm sorry I disappointed you."

He nodded, accepted the apology, then asked if I wanted to go out for breakfast. I took a deep breath and said yes.

◗

I could have begun this chapter with the clean glass windows reflecting the fall's afternoon sun back at me as I walked the streets of Coal Harbour. The obligatory first poutine scene, in which I marvel at the heavenly taste of salty fries covered in gravy and cheese curds. The mountain peaks drenched in clouds and dotted with snow and trees. The Sea to Sky Highway twirling around forests and islands in the dusk. The queer men walking hand in hand, or laughing unapologetically over brunch, or sending a woof on hookup apps.

I'd be lying if I said I never experienced these things. To be sure, there was a honeymoon period, days when I boarded the SkyTrain and got lost in the city without a guide, only to stumble upon English Bay or stroll aimlessly down a road covered in the fallen yellow leaves. When I filled in loved ones back home on the many wonders of Canada: the impossibly fast internet, the well-organized roads, the opera singer on the corner of Davie and Bute, the late-night bars on Granville Street. The easily accessible weed, delivered by a cute man on a bike with a huge backpack full of eighths and fourths, each strain with its own name and logo, its own purpose and outcome. The adorable dogs walking on steady leashes held by well-dressed men and women.

I could easily offer the familiar narrative that my troubles were forgotten the moment I landed in Canada, as if left in an unclaimed suitcase at Beirut International Airport. I could spin this movie-worthy yarn, ending the story at the arrivals gate of Vancouver International Airport, where I received hugs from all the white men I'd never met before welcoming me home to a place I'd never been. Roll the credits.

Instead, I'd rather tell you the truth.

For my first six months in Canada, Gary's presence dominated my life. At times I felt that I was in a non-consensual and emotionally abusive relationship. If I failed to report every step I made, I'd end up with a million texts and unannounced late-night visits. Gary was a master manipulator, with something negative to say about every-one I attempted to befriend. And if his warnings didn't work he'd act coy and hurt that I'd dared give my attention elsewhere. I had to sever every possible new connection so as not to tempt jealous fits and angry emails. Gary essentially lived in my apartment, oblivious to social cues to leave me alone and eventually refusing direct requests for privacy. Slowly, I lost my sense of self-determination. I didn't know who was making my decisions anymore.

I sometimes wonder why Gary fixated on me. Was it the glorious White Knight image he conjured every time we were together, seeing himself as the Saviour of Refugees, the Breaker of Chains? Did I legitimize him in front of his friends and colleagues? Render him more appealing? Was he in love the way Cee thought he was? In lust, maybe? Was he scared to be alone?

Or did the process of privately sponsoring a refugee create in him a sense of entitlement? Maybe he thought he was within his rights to steer me as he wished, like a brand-new yacht he'd bought with his hard-earned cash.

"This is Danny, my refugee," Gary said at one of the many fancy dinners he splurged on to get us into. I smiled and shook hands with people who spoke slower English to ensure I understood and then were stunned when I responded fluently. Never mind that I was technically no longer a refugee and had become a permanent resident of Canada the day of my arrival. Nor was I an object that belonged to him, like a piece of antique furniture.

I bit my tongue and said my hellos.

◖

In February, five months after my arrival in Vancouver, I was invited to speak at a storytelling event called Rain City Chronicles. The subject of this instalment was "the moment that changed your life."

"What are you going to talk about?" Gary asked, sitting on my couch while I stalled and pretended to clean something in the kitchen.

"It's a surprise," I said.

"Is it going to be a good surprise?"

"I think it will be. I wrote the piece last night."

"Do you want me to proofread it?" he asked, grabbing the laptop he'd bought me. "I don't mind taking a look."

I rushed to the living room and pulled the laptop out of his hand. I smiled and said that I'd rather keep it private for now. "It's still brewing, you know."

Backstage at the event, I rehearsed the lines over and over in my head until I heard my cue. I walked into the spotlight in my tight jeans and the velvet shirt Gary had given me from his closet.

Then I spoke about leaving Egypt.

I brought up Mia and the day the Egyptian revolution erupted. I spoke about the bear hug I felt around my waist and the hands that gathered on my body. The camera that I tried to protect with my life and the days that followed. The fear that grew in my heart every time I heard a protest outside. The brokenness I felt when I left Egypt. I had one hand balled into a fist in my pocket and the other holding onto the microphone. My nails dug into my sweaty palm and my heartbeat raced. I paused the way I'd practised; I cracked a joke just as planned. A final sigh. A quick thank you. A standing ovation. I tried to escape the stage but the show director told me to stay put until the applause cooled down. I bowed like a court jester. Then, when I raised my eyes, I saw Gary sitting in the front row, his arms crossed over his chest and a scowl on his face.

Gary trailed behind me as I left the stage, passing audience members who wanted to congratulate me on a job well done, shake my hand, or give me a hug.

"That was amazing," a tall man with a thick beard and blue eyes said. "You really came alive on that stage."

I'd noticed him in the front row from the stage and had rested my eyes on his handsome face once or twice, which helped me chill. "I enjoyed watching you watching me," I said, coming across flirtier than I'd intended. He asked me for my phone number.

"I think Danny is very tired," Gary jumped in, parting us with his body. "Shall we?" He grabbed my hand and rushed me to the door. We walked to the car without speaking.

"You seem mad," I said as he drove home, finally breaking the silence.

"I'm not mad." He adjusted his glasses on his nose. "I'm just surprised."

"Okay." Silence returned to the car, save for the patter of rain as Gary took a right onto Marine Drive.

"I just don't understand your choices," he said finally. "The theme was the day that changed your life, and you decide to talk about *Egypt*?"

"Well, if the revolution in Egypt never happened, I wouldn't have—"

"That's not what matters," he interrupted. "The day that changed your life was the day that I saved you!"

"Saved me?" I imagined Gary in military fatigues, knife between his teeth, jumping from an airplane with no parachute and releasing a primal scream into the Beirut skies. "Like in *Die Hard*?"

"Are you mocking me?"

"No," I said. "You're doing a fine job of that all on your own."

"You fucking ungrateful bitch." He swerved into the right-hand lane and came to an abrupt stop on the shoulder of the highway. The seat belt held my body from slamming into the dashboard. "If it weren't for me you'd be stuck in Beirut taking showers in sewage water."

"Gary, please drive." A truck honked at us as it zoomed by, narrowly missing the side mirror. "You'll get us both killed."

"You wear a watch I bought you and a shirt from my closet, and you live in an apartment I rented for you," he stammered. "And yet you can't even show me gratitude, bring me up on a stage like I deserve."

I cowered in my seat. "I'm sorry. I apologize. Can we drive now?"

He huffed in anger, weaved back into traffic, and remained silent throughout the rest of the trip. When we arrived at my place, I opened the car door.

"You're not going to even say good night?" he hissed.

"Good night!"

I rushed, shaking, into the apartment building. An hour later he showed up with a basket of oranges. "I was at the supermarket, and this made me think of you," he said. "Don't they smell delicious?"

◝

"I want to go back home," I said.

Mitch sat across the table from me, eyes wide. Chris, the founder of Rainbow Refugee, nodded next to him. We'd come to a downtown café for this emergency meeting while I was on my break from my mandatory language classes, which everyone agreed were a waste of time and resources.

"Don't say that, Danny," Mitch said.

"He won't leave me alone. I'm tired and overwhelmed. This is not what I signed up for. Canada looked better on paper, honestly."

Café patrons seemed to be looking at me, as I must have raised my voice without realizing it. Chris, wearing one of her signature colourful T-shirts, kept her eyes on me. She'd been a nun in her youth, before falling in love with a fellow sister and leaving the faith to travel the world fighting injustice. When they decided to settle in Canada in the early nineties, they discovered that the law allowing Canadians to sponsor their foreign partners was designed only for heterosexual couples. Chris, ever the shit disturber, took the federal government to court and managed to change the law. This was the seed case from which Rainbow Refugee grew. Over the years, hundreds of folks identifying as LGBTQ+ had been brought into Canada through Chris's work.

"That's your decision if you want to make it," she said, her voice calm and collected. "There are less drastic measures we can take, though."

"Like what?" I was shaking. I'd smoked a couple of joints that morning, hoping they'd steady my voice. Instead I felt as if warmth was seeping out of my limbs and that I had to protect it in my core. My broken rib ached. I tightened my arms around my chest.

"Well, I can have a meeting with him to relieve him of his role as your sponsor and take your case under the direct supervision of the Rainbow Refugee board," she explained.

"He'll show up shouting and screaming at my door!"

"Then you move. Mitch will help you find a place elsewhere," Chris said. "Hell, you can move to a different city or another province if you want."

I didn't want to move to a different province. I'd just been offered a job at Qmunity, a non-profit organization that offers services to the LGBTQ2S+ communities in B.C.

"I want to move downtown," I told them. Mitch promised to help me find an apartment near the Village.

"Danny, you look quite thin," Chris said before giving me a bone-crushing hug. "Take care of yourself, kid. Don't let the world eat you."

A few days after I started at Qmunity, its executive director, Dara, called me to her office.

"I want to ask you about a man who came to my office today," she said. "We received a five-hundred-dollar donation from him two days ago, and as we usually do, I invited him out for coffee."

As Dara told me of her meeting with Gary, I froze, unable to breathe. Overnight, I had packed and moved to an apartment on Georgia Street, near the Village, walking distance from my new workplace. I'd blocked Gary across social media and ignored the dozens of emails he sent at all hours of the day. Lengthy ones dissecting every conversation we'd ever had. Short ones bursting with anger over how I had supposedly conned him. Single-sentence ones implying that he was considering suicide. A text at four in the morning begging me to pick up the phone.

"He spent the hour telling me about you," Dara said. "He claimed that you were having mental health issues and that the only way to support you would be for me to fire you so that you could return to his care."

I bit my lower lip and listened.

"Do you know this guy, Danny?" she asked. "He said he knows you."

I burst. I cried like a fucking baby, gasping for air, sobbing fat wet tears, moaning like a wounded soldier. Dara asked me to sit down and came to my side, holding my hand and waiting till I stopped, what was likely twenty minutes, silently handing me tissue after tissue.

"Tell me what's going on," she said when I finally calmed down. Words shot out my mouth like bullets from a machine gun. I wasn't even sure I was making sense, but I kept talking. I told her about the drive home from the storytelling event, about my arrest in Damascus, and the salty water in Beirut. I told her how broken I felt, like a smashed mosaic, pieces scattered everywhere and impossible to put back together. I begged her not to fire me. "I need this job," I said. "I need to be able to afford life on my own here. I am good for it, I swear it."

"I'm not going to fire you," she said. She returned to her desk. "I want to hire you a lawyer. Is that okay with you?"

"A lawyer?"

"You need to create clear and lawful boundaries with this man," she said. "A lawyer can help you get a peace bond."

"What's that?"

She scrolled through her contacts until she landed on one. "It's like a restraining order," she said. "I have a good friend who's a lawyer. I'm sure I can get her to volunteer her time. Do you want me to call her?"

"Yes."

Dara got her friend on the phone, and after quickly narrating the story, she gave her my contact info. The matter was now in the lawyer's capable hands.

For days, Gary pretended not to be home to avoid receiving a letter from my lawyer. He finally signed it when the delivery clerk caught him outside his apartment at an early hour. But even after that he appeared a couple times across the street from my new apartment, standing by the traffic light, staring me down. And he emailed once more, swearing that he'd gone to therapy and that the doctor had asked him to get in touch with me to iron things out for his own mental health. I blocked him, but the emails kept arriving from different accounts. Finally I created a new email address and abandoned my old inbox.

In his last email he sent me a picture of Robin Williams, a childhood hero of mine who'd died of suicide, and wrote: "I saved you. Why can't you save me?"

The heaviness of the decision not to respond still aches in my side.

●

"Sheesh, are you okay? That sounds horrendous."

I was telling my coworker Alex about the Gary situation over lunch at the best sushi restaurant on Davie Street. They were the closest thing to a friend I'd made at Qmunity. A non-binary trans person of South Asian descent, they took me under their wing, answering all my questions about life in Canada and filling me in on topics I was only just coming to learn about: non-binary identity, preferred pronouns, self-care. I'd opened up to them about feeling too queer to join the Syrian community here, fearing that the immigrant community in Vancouver had imported homophobic beliefs from back in Syria.

"I'm totally fine," I said. But it was far from the truth: I hadn't been sleeping well, and a growing sense of dread permeated my days. "He's such a crazy person."

"Crazy is a bad term," they explained. Alex was thoughtful. They held their words in their mouth and flipped them around until they were in the right order. "It just speaks to a degradation of mental health issues. Try wild, unimaginable. Maybe terrible. He sounds like a terrible person."

I laughed. "Terrible won't cut it. We need a new word for that guy."

"Racist would do just fine," they said.

"Oh, that's a stretch."

"Is it though?"

"I mean the guy is terrible," I said. "I'm not in the business of defending him. But racist?"

"Here's the issue," Alex began. "There was no balance in that relationship. There was a power struggle. He is a white man, Canadian, older, with financial power over you, who abused his power and mistreated you. You are a person of colour, with an immigration status, who was placed in a system in which you depended on him.

"The system is flawed. Creating sponsorships by circles of Canadians to bring in immigrants who are mainly POCs, then expecting the Canadians—the majority of whom will be white—to understand the power dynamic and protect the self-determination of the immigrant? It saves lives, but with the wrong sponsor, as in your case, we're putting immigrants in a dangerous and deprivileged position."

"But there are thousands of refugees seeking safety in Canada," I said, "and only dozens of volunteers willing to take on the sponsorship role."

"More reason we need to offer these folks training to ensure the newly arriving refugees have the best support they deserve," Alex said.

The problem with this narrative, I explained to Alex, was that my identity as a person of colour—a new term I was still navigating— seemed to bring me only disadvantages: stereotypes that associated my legal name with that of Islamic terrorists, discrimination that prevented me from getting jobs, and second-degree profiling at airports. "My brownness will never be a good thing," I said.

"That's because you're always comparing your brown skin to whiteness, Danny. Try separating your racial identity from the system we live under. What makes you proud of your identities? What makes you value yourself? What aspects of your heritage and culture are you comfortable incorporating into your everyday life and which ones would you rather let go? You get to be the engineer of your racial identity, and that's beautiful."

Over the next months I would make a point of learning more—in libraries and online—about what it means to be Syrian, a descendant of the Assyrian kingdom, which ruled the region thousands of years ago: its traditions remaining despite the years, mixing themselves with Islamic practices and cultural norms. I would learn to appreciate the way my brown skin shimmered under the sun, goldened under its rays. I would learn to recognize my privilege as a man, realize my power as a queer person, and celebrate my heritage as a Syrian.

The more I got to know this person I was becoming, the less pressure I felt in my chest. The journey to overcome my past traumas, however, was only just beginning.

BREAKTHROUGH

It was May 2015, and the sun had broken through the clouds for the first time in months: a welcome sign for someone who constantly felt he'd had a yawn stuck in the back of his throat.

I invited some friends over for a dollar store party: we would raid the nearby Dollarama for cheap masks, feathered boas, and plastic hats, then gather at my home, get stoned and dance.

There was something happening to me, and I couldn't fully understand it yet. I'd finally finished my three-month training period and secured my full-time job at Qmunity, meaning I was now financially independent and so could leave the private refugee sponsorship early. No more oversight from sponsors, whether of the stable or stalker variety. Summer was around the corner, promising an end to the rainy Vancouver days. Pride was a couple months away, and I'd be marching in the parade with my coworkers. I was happy, or at least I looked it from the outside. This was the life I'd been promised, and now I was living it. The city that celebrated Pride, the home near the gay village, the job at a local community centre.

Yet, when I sat alone with my thoughts, I felt them ganging up on me. I floated on the surface of my consciousness, attempting not to make a sound, while my emotions circled like sharks. *Inhale, exhale*, I told myself, *everything will be fine*. Guilt, unreasonable and unsourced, gnawed at my thigh. The muscle jolted; the nerve tensed. Dread, appearing out of thin air like a menacing ghost, grabbed my shoulders and tightened them together. A memory of pain echoed off my body, guiding my fingers to my lower back. I pressed with all my might, hoping to return a muscle or a bone to its original location.

I channelled my energy toward pressing hard on these thoughts. I imagined squeezing them all into a pressure cooker in my brain and tightening its lid. The pot shook, and steam escaped. The shaking left my brain and found its way down to my fingers and toes. I cracked my knuckles and tapped my feet on the ground, the way my mother did after she took her meds and could no longer scream her anxieties into the wind.

We returned victorious from the dollar store with a shiny red plastic fireman's helmet, a hairband with bunny ears, countless colourful beaded Mardi Gras necklaces—a subsequent photo shoot was all but guaranteed. My British friend, married to a Syrian woman, wore a cheaply made jacket covered in four-leaf clovers and assumed an Irish accent. I was tasked with rolling the joints.

My weed was stashed in a butter cookie tin, just like what my grandmother had used for her extra sewing needles and thread. I sifted through the baggies, deciding on a strain.

"Which one did you roll last time?" a friend asked.

"Lemon Haze."

"That one." He sounded like a kid in a candy store. "That one was fire!"

Lemon Haze it was. I picked at the flower expertly and inserted its pieces into my grinder, then twisted it, inhaling the green smell.

With the rolling papers folded between my fingers, I gently tipped the opened grinder to let the shredded leaves flicker in. Then I rolled a small, thin piece of cardboard for the filter and anchored the joint into it before screwing the top shut. I also had a purple and orange pipe that I'd been given as a birthday gift, but I preferred joints; they reminded me of back home.

"Ready, boys?" We rode the elevator down to the second floor and stepped into the parking lot. It was golden hour, and everything looked magnificent. We sat on the fence, lit the joint, and passed it around.

Someone pulled their phone out and took a picture of me. I avoided looking directly into the lens. My hair was messy under my toque, my beard untrimmed, my eyes empty of sparkle. "Smile, why don't you?" he said. I smirked, and he took another.

Afterward we huddled back into the elevator, where I struggled to press the right buttons. We laughed a bit too much over such a silly thing. Back in my apartment, music played and people danced. Someone opened a bottle of wine and I poured myself a glass. I sat back with my head high and tried to focus, but my vision was blurred.

It scared me that I couldn't focus.

I've got to keep sharp, I thought. *I've got to stay on my best behaviour. You never know when the world will decide to betray you once again. You never know when the next big thing will happen. I have to protect myself, and in order to do so, I have to be aware of everything. But the world is prickly, and without the weed it bleeds everywhere.*

I took a deep breath.

Why can't my eyes focus? Why is my breathing so loud? How do my fingers move? My beard is itchy. Did I touch a cat? I'm allergic to cats. Why am I allergic to cats in Canada but not in Syria? My arm is itchy, too. Is that a bug bite?

I scratched my forearm until dots of blood appeared. I downed the last of the wine like water.

Jesus turned wine to water. Or was it water to wine? The music is too loud; the neighbours will call the police. I'm so sorry officer, we didn't realize, I'll turn it down right away. I am so sorry officer, we didn't realize it was so loud, I will turn it down right away. I am so sorry officer, we didn't—

"Are you okay?" The British guy was sitting next to me.

"Oh yeah." I massaged my face with both hands, pressing hard on my temples, then running my palms down my cheeks and feeling the tips of my fingers on my lower lip. "Why wouldn't I be?"

The question echoed in my skull. My neck got tighter, as if my upper back were trying to swallow my head. I pressed hard at my shoulders to loosen them.

"Hey, easy on your body," he said.

I avoided eye contact.

Breathing through my nose became harder. I swallowed, then parted my lips to take air in. I heard my breath wheeze loudly inside my head, out of sync with my thumping heart.

"Danny, you okay?" he asked again.

When I finally looked at his face, all I could see were his crooked teeth.

I felt as though I'd been slapped. My heartbeat quickened and my breathing got shallower. Thoughts scrambled in my head as if they were once neatly placed Scrabble tiles and someone had just flipped the board. My brain refused to focus.

It took all my might to blink. Then, for a millisecond, I was in the dark place, and it felt as painful as a cracked rib, as lonely as a final goodbye.

"I am so sorry," I said.

"Why are you sorry?"

"I am staring." My vision was laser-focused. I couldn't see my friend's eyes, his red cheeks, his large nose, his shaggy brown hair. I couldn't see anything but his crooked teeth, large enough in my vision as if I'd zoomed in on them. I squeezed my eyes shut, shook my head, then looked again. Our eyes met, and he smiled.

"Danny, are you stoned?" he joked. His teeth appeared once more, and my vision caught them. The tunnel was tight and I was in the middle of it. The moment stretched; time itself stopped moving to witness it.

"I just need some water." I tried to stand, but it felt as if I'd sunk deeper into the sofa. I pushed with my arms and tightened my glutes, and finally I was vertical again. My heart raced and my limbs felt heavy. Every muscle in my body tightened. My vision doubled, as if my eyes were crossed. Pressure in my fingers and toes, burning in my chest. I'd never experienced a boiling of the blood until now. My veins were so hot I could trace them with my fingers, even the ones deep within my body. I held it together and cracked a smile, then said something.

"Huh?"

I repeated myself.

"You're too damn high, you're speaking nonsense."

"Word salad!" said another voice.

"I'm sorry." I finally found the words. "I'm so thirsty."

My head was under the faucet. The water was lukewarm but I didn't care; I gulped it as if I'd just run a marathon. Streams trickled through my beard and down my T-shirt. When I stopped, everyone was looking at me. I ducked off to the bathroom, shut the door behind me, and leaned against the sink. The music was still loud, but I could tell the boys had stopped dancing and begun to murmur instead. In the mirror, my left eye drifted away from the right.

"Danny, are you okay?" asked a voice from outside.

"Yes. Yeah, I'm totally fine." My left eye, as if afraid of being noticed, returned to its normal location. I stared at my reflection, trying to catch the eye attempting another escape. It stayed where it was. I kept staring. I stared some more. *It'll happen any minute now. Just you wait.* I pulled my phone out, pressed record, and filmed myself staring at my reflection, then sat on the toilet and examined the footage. Nothing: the left eye eluded being caught in the act.

"Danny, you've been in there for half an hour," a voice said. "Come out already."

Half an hour? I looked at my phone, but the numbers were tangled and unintelligible.

"Coming!" I announced. I opened the bathroom door and smiled.

●

Okay, reader—I need to let you in on a little secret. I want to tell my story with authority, but I think we can all admit that memories warp and stretch. Holes are left, needing to be filled. I could have written everything exactly as I remember it, but that version would be riddled with qualified statements and uncertainties. One thing I can say for certain is true: I am triggered by the sight of crooked teeth. So, I peppered this narrative with them.

Were the teeth of the dead man in the YouTube video crooked? I couldn't say for sure. The officer in Damascus who asked me to spy on my people? If I'm honest, I can't recall his face. My elementary-school crush who needed braces? I wouldn't be able to pick him out of a lineup.

You see, the fiction writer in me couldn't handle leaving you with ambiguity. I would rather keep you captivated by well-crafted scenes and dialogue. I'd rather stitch motifs together—crooked teeth, shy smiles, playful bites—than lecture you on trauma, racial injustice, and the refugee crisis.

I'm telling you these stories as I would tell them to a friend. Sure, I might be misremembering, filling some gaps with innocent embellishments, but my delivery is full of certainty and my story is full of meaning. You could check every fact like a journalist, or you could feel the story the way I did, let its truth speak to your heart.

I had my first post-traumatic stress disorder trigger during a dollar store party. I didn't know to call it a trigger then. My head was filled with so much anxiety that I couldn't think rationally or articulate what was happening to me. When the attacks happen, my face feels as if it's been struck by lightning. The whole world goes silent. I freeze. Then, an ache in my forehead, the kind of pain that makes me want to vomit. My thought processes halt, and instead I struggle to find my place in my own stream of consciousness.

Imagine it like this: Life is a steady river, and you float softly on its surface. Suddenly the current picks up and you slip under.

For a moment you struggle to tell up from down; you get tangled in seaweed. You start to fear for your life and you flail your arms around. Your clothing snags on a rock on the riverbed and you unintentionally injure yourself trying to wriggle loose. Then your head pops above the surface and you take a deep breath. It takes you a second to remember how shallow this river is and how steady you can be if you just stand up; the water isn't even deep enough to wet your shirt.

Triggers aren't like what you see in the movies: They don't follow a coherent path, transporting you neatly back to a certain time and space. At least for me, they bring out a mixture of feelings that have no connection to the current moment. The fear of isolation, the stress of imprisonment, the brokenness of physical pain, and a half memory of somewhere else, usually untethered to a situation or logic.

Attempting to rationalize a trigger is a fool's errand.

My counsellor, an Indigenous woman who ran a clinic in her art studio, said that the human brain is like a muscle with a specific capacity. Under too much weight it snaps. When it heals, it's left with a scar but also a higher capacity. The term *mental breakdown*, borrowed from whatever vocabulary I had to describe my mother's illnesses, swam around our sessions, but she insisted that I abandon it. "A mental breakthrough," she said, "is a way for you to expand beyond the shackles of your story into who you ought to be right now."

"Fluffy bullshit," I joked, sitting back in a comfortable chair, constantly checking the time.

"Maybe it is." She laughed. "But that's what we'll call it from now on."

Is my obsession with teeth some animal instinct hidden in my lizard brain since birth? A remnant from back when humanity was crawling out of the forests and learning how to make fire? Cave dwellers chewed on sticks and bones to clean their teeth and used grass to pick between their molars. Were they sharpening their natural weapons? A last resort if arrows and axes failed? I've watched enough *CSI* to know that each human has a unique bitemark. Teeth keep our history for us, engraved in those exposed bones.

Dogs bare their teeth to show aggression. They growl at one another and present their strength, their danger. Monkeys protect their young until their offspring have all their teeth, then off to the wilderness they go to fend for themselves. Teeth pierce the skin of an apple, clean meat off a bone. Is my obsession with them a desire to consume a world intent on chewing me up and spitting me out? When I kiss someone, I tend to bite their lips. I leave marks on their shoulders and upper arms. I'm aroused when I see the indentations my teeth have left on someone else's skin. Am I simply too hungry for their affection?

Teeth grow to accomplish a noble function: to feed the body they belong to. Even the crooked ones. They still feed, bite, protect. They still take space. They still offer pleasure. Yet we have an aversion to them, a preoccupation with fixing them. People will endure painful and expensive surgeries to set them straight or to replace them with shiny veneers. Is my fixation some sort of replacement grief over growing up the crooked tooth in my family, guilt over refusing to be straightened or over how willingly I uprooted myself?

"This question is unanswerable," my counsellor said. "There's no way for us to understand a trigger. It just is. It's a symptom of your PTSD."

"How do I stop it, then?"

"You don't stop it, you flow with it," she said.

My mind is the sky, she explained. It's the moon and the sun and the stars. The rocks that fly aimlessly in dark cold space, the comets with long tails roaming on their forever paths. My emotions, on the other hand, are the weather. They are the sunny day filled with warmth and the cloudy day that requires a cup of tea. They are the sudden thunderstorms and the deep gurgle of snow-heavy clouds.

When it rains or snows, I remain the sky. The sun need not worry itself with clouds. The moon is unaffected by tsunamis and hurricanes. I function through my weathered emotions but remain steady in my own body. I separate my triggers from my sense of self, and I find the real me. I remain here: a space filled with wonder. A universe.

I still get triggered sometimes, though not as much as I did back then. I pause mid-sentence and my eyes narrow into tunnel vision. I get stuck on crooked teeth and my heart sinks into my stomach. You might see me laugh awkwardly or stumble on my words. You might notice me taking a deep breath or mumbling a funny sentence over and over. I might excuse myself and walk away unceremoniously. I learned how to be fine with these moments. How to accept these minor embarrassments and not feel the need to apologize for them.

My trigger was the faces of those I couldn't remember, the pains of those I left behind, and the sorrow that my life couldn't go in a straight line. My trigger was the officer in the airport, the man in the Mukhabarat basement, my mother's face crying in her bedroom, and the tip of a machine gun.

My trigger is what it is. It has always been. There is no ending it. There is only learning to navigate it.

NOW

Is there an ending when it comes to writing a memoir? Here is a present continuous instead.

VANCOUVER

Today I become Canadian, or so I've been promised. I am once again handed a number. The Canadian Immigration and Citizenship officer smiles as she confirms the dates with me. Four years in Canada. Then she shows me my papers.

"This is your seat number," she explains. "You can't sit at any random seat. Do you understand that?"

"Yes." I grab my papers.

"Is that a wedding ring?" she asks. "It's beautiful."

"Engagement." I smile gingerly, glancing at the ring, a fusion of wood and gold.

"Your future wife has good taste," she says.

"Well, I picked it for myself and my future husband," I say. Matthew, sitting with the friends who've come to witness the occasion, smiles when he catches me eyeing him.

I've just given up my permanent residency card, alongside my travel document, in exchange for a piece of paper promising me a citizenship certificate and the ability to apply for a Canadian passport after the ceremony. There is a hint of illogical panic growing within me. If the earth came to a halt now, I would be homeless. A stateless person once again. Sweat gathers between my shoulder blades, just as it had back in the UNHCR offices. "That's it?"

"Yes. Now you join the swear-in ceremony," she says. "Congrats again, both on your upcoming wedding and your citizenship today."

I return to my seat next to Matthew. The room is large, its walls covered in posters of Canadian attractions and government-support programs. It's striking that the majority of those around us are people of colour. A nervous family of Asian descent huddles together after herding their children to their seats. A young Latino man sits by himself, next to a Black couple who've been holding hands since the moment they set foot in the hall.

"We got you something," my friend Natalie says, offering me a basket filled with maple cream cookies, a couple of small Canadian flags, and a pin for my lapel. I'm genuinely moved. I affix the pin to my blazer and bite into a cookie. Moments later, a uniformed officer invites all those swearing their citizenship oath to the courtroom next door.

"You'll be separated from your guests," the officer says. "They can witness you from the gallery while you sit in your designated seat."

Cee, who rarely gets visibly emotional, wraps his arms around me and holds me tight. "Don't fuck up your oath," he says.

"I love you, you silly thing," I whisper.

My friends line up to hug me as if I were setting off on a journey to a faraway land. Natalie kisses me on both cheeks. Her husband, Jason, shakes my hand and pulls me in for a bear hug. Alex, her teenage son who's looked up to me since the day we met, makes a joke. Her shy and quiet daughter, Maddie, tells me to break a leg. Mitch, one of the sponsors who facilitated my arrival in Canada, tears up when he tells me how proud he is to witness this moment. Bradley, Samantha, and JP have all dressed up for the occasion. Janie drove all the way downtown, a rare occurrence. Maggie, Matthew's mother, says it was all meant to be. Myriam hands me a tissue to dab my tears. "What tears?" I ask, before I feel the heat on my cheeks.

I intertwine my fingers with Matthew's, and we walk together to the courtroom. We will repeat this walk nine months later on our wedding day, the same group of friends escorting us like an entourage. We hold on to each other until it is finally time to separate. He asks if I'm ready.

"I'm still mad I have to swear allegiance to the queen," I tease.

"Oh, give it up already."

I find my seat just in time for the ceremony to begin. The lights dim and a projector screen slides down behind the empty judge's podium. A familiar blue box appears, with a white *Insert DVD* prompt in its corner, then a promotional video about the beauty and diversity of Canada plays.

"Oh my god. This is so cheesy," I whisper to the person sitting next to me, who says nothing. The video shows beautiful landscapes set to an upbeat orchestral melody. The typical views: the mountains and the oceans, the cliffs and the frozen lakes. A First Nations person dancing in traditional regalia, an interracial couple holding a baby. A Pride parade led by a drag queen. Suddenly there are rivers down my cheeks. I get mad at myself: If this is so cheesy, why is it burning my chest like desire? Why does it feel as certain as stone? I rely on my years of therapy and decide not to judge or dismiss my feelings. *I deserve this*, I think; *I worked hard for it. I suffered enough for it.* The tears won't stop.

Myriam makes her way through the rows of seats, inviting dirty looks from the guards, and hands me another tissue. "I love you," she whispers.

"Go back to your seat." I fight the urge to curl into a ball and hide.

The video ends and the bailiff announces the judge's arrival. My mind wants to blur the ceremony away, but I focus it to be present. I want to remember every second of this, to keep it for those days when I'd question where I was and who I'd become. I want to keep this day like a string tied around my wrist. I listen intently to the words of the judge, acknowledging the First Nations land we are on, inviting people to consider their privilege in becoming Canadian, and to see their journey to make it here. She locks eyes with me, I am sure of it. She sees my tears and smiles. Finally she stands, and everyone rises with her. We repeat the oath after her, both in English and in French. When we are done, she welcomes us to becoming Canadian. The court applauds politely. The national anthem plays and we all sing along. The new Canadians line up to receive their citizenship papers. When it's my turn I extend a hand to the judge and she passes me my certificate.

The whole room looks at my twelve guests as they cheer, applaud, pump their fists, and wave their flags.

Today I am finally home.

DAMASCUS

I'll be schmoozing tonight. I schmooze now; it's a thing.

My nerves always get the best of me before an event, but I have my defences. I wear the mosaic bandana Bradley got me from the Syrian section at Dubai Expo 2020. It's soft against my neck and partly underneath my pink wedding shirt. I wear the bowtie Dima got me on her last visit to Damascus. She held on to it for three years until I managed to visit her in London, post-pandemic. My new shoes, white with the rainbow flag on their soles. I wink at the mirror. I practise smiling and cocking an eyebrow in surprise. The charms are on. My armour is ready: I am now capable of schmoozing.

"Stop stressing. Everything will go according to plan," Cee says as I exit the bathroom. We walk toward the event hall together. He'll be the point of contact for volunteers while I do the call to action. He'll pass along the clipboards with the donation forms and ensure that everyone who wants to donate with cash or credit is served properly.

"Who said anything about stress?" It takes me a second to steady my voice. Cee smirks.

The hall has been transformed over the past three hours. Bradley, Matthew's bestie and one of my closest friends, works in set design. He's turned this boring wedding hall into a Damascene oasis, complete with a fountain in its centre. I'd left a few oranges and apples there, just as my grandmother used to do in Damascus. There are low and comfortable wooden chairs with purple and orange cushions, framed pictures from Damascus on the walls, and platters of delicious food cooked by a group of Syrian refugee women. The finishing touch is a cheeky sign by the door in the style of a traffic indicator.

Damascus 10,594 KM.

I created this annual event eight years ago. It started in a small home and gathered around a hundred people. My friends and I cooked Syrian food, decorated the house, and invited people over. To our delight, we raised five thousand dollars. Today the event is sponsored by one of the biggest banks in Canada and raises a good forty thousand dollars annually for Rainbow Refugee.

"It's almost six o'clock," Cristie says. She was our wedding planner and volunteers her time for this event every year. "Are we all ready?"

I run through the list in my head: Volunteer orientation, check. Practised speech, check. Drag queens—technically late, but here in due time—check. The American Sign Language interpreters, check. Our sponsors' merch and logos displayed, check. The Evening in Damascus is ready to roll. I nod to Cristie, who rushes over to let the volunteers at the registration table know. The doors open. Schmoozing time.

Over the next twenty minutes, three hundred guests walk through the large wooden gates of the event hall. They marvel at the photographs and the fountain. They use their drink tickets at the bar in the corner and peruse the auction items spread on a table to the side. The photo booth is busy: we printed a replica of the Umayyad Mosque's courtyard as a backdrop and stationed a drag queen there to take photos with the guests. It tickles me to see a drag performer sassing the attendees against a backdrop of one of Islam's holiest sites.

"You look good," Bradley whispers as he passes me. "Don't stress."

I chuckle. My friends know me too well. I softly touch his arm as he walks away.

The crowd gathers, and a Syrian oud player fills the room with the music of his strings. There is joy in this room, I can feel it. The space is charged with laughter and warm embraces. Happiness, I have learned, fades. It's a chemical reaction that floods your brain with an instant gratification. Serotonin rarely lingers. Joy, on the other hand, is an immortal feeling. It's what I feel for my accomplishments over the past eight years in Canada, for being able to pull myself up and make this fundraiser happen. This will live forever. This will last. I smile a genuine smile to myself.

"Here you are," Samantha says. Matthew and I met her when she volunteered at the event five years ago; we became fast friends. "I need you to sign your new novel for me."

Since meeting, we've travelled to Mexico, Egypt, and the U.K. together, and we plan to add Latin America and Thailand to the list in the coming years. A fellow book nerd, Samantha became my loyal first reader. She read *The Foghorn Echoes* even before I sent it to my editor.

"Anything for you, love." Her fiery red hair smells of jasmine.

"Great. I have twenty-six copies in a box in the volunteer room."

"Twenty-six?"

"Yeah," she says with a smile. "I have a lot of friends."

I promise to sign the books after the event and leave her with two of her own guests. Matthew winks at me from a corner. He's a master schmoozer, grabbing the attention of a full circle of strang-ers, narrating funny stories and making smart observations. His hair bounces when he laughs and his eyes twinkle. Later tonight, when everything is said and done, I will rest my tired body on our queen-size bed and Matthew will kiss me good night. Our dog will snuggle in between us and the two of them will fall asleep instantly, like a spell of magic. Their snores will fill the bedroom like a noise machine. It will be a blessing.

"Excuse me," says a small voice from behind me. Schmoozing time. "Are you Danny?"

"Yes, I am." I turn with my practised smile. Standing there is a petite woman in a pretty dress. Her hair is wavy and dark, her eyes black as the night sky. She smiles and places a shy hand on my shoulder.

"I just wanted to say thank you," she says, inviting in a second petite woman who seems reluctant to join our circle. "*We* wanted to thank you."

"Of course, my love. I hope you're enjoying your night. Did you see the fountain?" I say, relying on a line I've already repeated once or twice this evening.

"I just want to say," she continues, "we're so thankful you put this event together. We arrived three months ago in Canada as newcom-ers from the Middle East. It's a struggle, you know. It's been really difficult. When they told me you offered us free tickets, we didn't even know we wanted to come, but the program coordinator insisted."

I donate free tickets to local non-profit organizations that ser-vice the queer and trans refugee communities in Vancouver, with the mindset that I don't want a room full of old white men. I also want the event to be a place for queer and trans newcomers to enjoy—we usually end up with around thirty of them every year.

My attitude shifts. This is not a schmooze. I turn toward her fully and step forward to create a smaller safe space for her to speak. Her friend joins our little huddle. We whisper.

"I didn't know that this could happen," she says, switching to Arabic. "I didn't know that we could have a space like this. This feels like home, Danny. Thank you for inviting us."

She explains that she met her girlfriend in an Arab country where queerness is punished by death. The two fled and had been on the road for years until Rainbow Refugee brought them to Canada.

"When we landed in Vancouver, everything was frightening," she says. "They tell you that when you come here you will feel safe. But I haven't felt safe since I landed. I feel that everything is new and different and strange."

"Because it is," I whisper back. The noise of chattering guests becomes muted, as if it's just the three of us in the room. "Those frightening moments are real, because you feel them. You're embarking on a new journey, and that can be scary. But you're allowed to be scared and brave at the same time, my friend."

She nods. Her girlfriend comes closer till we're all shoulder to shoulder. I hunch slightly to their height.

"When I walked into this room it felt possible that I could make it one day. That we can make it together one day. You uplifted us. Thank you." She holds on to my hand. Her girlfriend, finally making eye contact, softly touches my shoulder. Then the two of them disappear into the crowd, and I'm left floored.

"You're due on stage," Cristie whispers in my ear.

"I think I need a minute." I rush to the bathroom and into a stall. *I'm not going to cry*, I repeat to myself. Tears gather in my eyes and I dab them with a square of toilet paper. I compose myself, head back out, and spend the next three hours acting as emcee, introducing drag queens and belly dancers, opening the buffet with olive oil–drenched salads and sautéed lemon chicken, and cueing up speeches by folks I've handpicked for this event. There's laughter, some tears. By the end of the night over sixty thousand dollars will have been raised for Rainbow Refugee, our largest donation yet.

I never see the two petite women again. I don't even know their names. But I'm grateful for having met them. It was all worth it, just for that moment. To be able to offer this space is a gift. It makes me feel that I'm doing what I was born to do.

LOVE

It's 2018, and Matthew and I are in Paris.

We agree that we have only one day to visit the Louvre, leaving us with two options: either rush through it like the wind, taking a quick look at every single corner, or choose our targeted sections and accept that we'll have to come back to Paris and finish the tour in the future. A marathon or a meander, no in between. We decide to meander.

We hold hands and walk around as if we own the place, taking photos in the glorious light gathered by the inverted pyramid. We slip into the café on a balcony overlooking the French gardens and have an espresso with a delicate biscuit. We avoid the tourists running through the museum in groups. Some flash their cameras, angering the security guard, who berates them in French and leaves them confused. We reach the Aphrodite sculpture, swarmed by tourists, some even using their iPads to film it.

"Who uses an iPad for its camera?" I ask, and Matthew giggles.

We landed in the U.K. earlier that week before crossing the channel to Paris. After deplaning at the airport, we reached an arrow directing Canadians and Australians to a specific door.

"What do I do now?" I asked Matthew.

"Scan your passport." He showed me first. The doors opened for him and he slipped to the other side. I grabbed my Canadian passport, pristine and shiny, and scanned it, too. The glass door opened and I stepped onto British lands. We walked down the hall, then turned the corner to see the baggage carousel.

"Wait!"

"What?"

"There's no security?" I asked. "Did I miss a step? No one asked me anything. Is it that easy?"

"You're Canadian now, you don't need visas," he said, absent-mindedly watching the belt for our luggage. He looked back and saw me standing still. "What's up?"

"I never thought this would ever happen." My experience of airports was being interrogated and arrested for no apparent reason. I was used to the assumptions and the dirty looks. I was used to being forced to empty my pockets.

At the Louvre, we reach the destination I've always wanted to see: the Assyrian section in the basement. In the nineteenth century French archaeologists excavated a palace in the unfinished city of Khorsabad in what was once the Assyrian Empire and is now Iraq. Still mostly intact, the buildings had stood for hundreds of years. The French thought it was a good idea to pack up the city as it was, transport it, then rebuild it. I stand in awe before the two tall, mighty statues that guarded its gate, tilting my head up to take in their entirety. Walking the hallways, surrounded by the walls of my ancestors, I feel at peace. I want to touch the stones and smell their dust, but I'm stopped by my sense of care for these historic remains, not to mention the panes of glass and polite velvet ropes.

"Hey, can you stand here?" Matthew asks. He pulls his phone out and points it at me. "Yeah. Cross your arms. Great. Lift up your chin a bit. Yes. Now, look to the centre, right at the camera." I hear the clicking noise. "Come see this."

He flips his phone around and I see the photo of me in front of the Assyrian statue with the body of a lion and the head of a man. The beard is braided like children's hair and the smile is mischievous, as if the statue knows something we all do not.

"Look closer," Matthew says.

The statue and I have the same nose, the same high cheekbones and eyebrows. We have the same eyes and even the same smile. My beard, although shorter, looks just as wild. "If there was ever doubt that you're Assyrian . . ." Matthew remarks.

"It looks like a statue of a lost uncle," I say.

That night, naked in our tiny hotel room in Paris, I decide that I'm going to marry this man.

Sixteen years after our first meeting, it's Sama I text when I'm about to propose to Matthew. Months after Paris, I stand in my home in Vancouver, across the globe from Sama, putting the final touches on my outfit. Syrian sherwal pants, a red fez, and a colourful vest matched with a traditional belt someone smuggled out of Damascus for me. I take a photo.

What do you think? It's past midnight in Turkey, but Sama is a night owl.

Looking sharp! she texts back. *Ready for your event?*

I think so.

I still struggle sometimes to create a connection between my mind and my heart. My mind has learned, after years of therapy, that I am worthy of love. It had its training and graduated with flying colours; I understand that I—with my soft touch and expansive mind and creative soul—am worthy of adoration and care. My heart, however, sometimes falls a few steps behind; it forgets, nags all afternoon for affirmations, and aches for past pains it couldn't forgive.

On such occasions Matthew holds my hand, brings me closer, and asks if I want chocolate.

Did you get the ring? The velvet box is hidden in my closet behind my folded shirts. I slip it into my backpack while Matthew's in the bathroom. Matthew loves gold, and I prefer wood, so a friend found a wedding band from Hawaii that perfectly marries the two. Everyone we know has planned to be there at my annual Evening in Damascus fundraiser.

Do you know what you'll say?

I have a general idea, I write back. *I am very nervous, Sama. What if he says no?*

Then he's stupid. No one says no to my daughter. You are smart, handsome, and successful. If he says no, it's his loss.

You're such a mother-in-law already.

I check myself in the mirror one last time: It's not lost on me that I'll be proposing to a man while wearing a traditional Syrian outfit. My Damascene roots and my queerness have come together in a beautiful harmony.

You know, if I asked Rainbow Refugee to sponsor you to come to Canada, they will help in a heartbeat, I write Sama. The text bubble appears, indicating that she's typing her response, then it disappears, then reappears.

Why would I ever leave Turkey? I have my home here, and a gaggle of girls who live with me. Business is going well. I'm living like a queen.

I send her a heart emoji.

Sponsor someone else, child. Some trans girl living in a refugee camp.

Okay, Mother, I reply. I stare at the screen for a moment, then turn off my phone. Shoes laced, shirt ironed, bag filled, speeches prepared. I stand by the door and wait for Matthew.

"You ready to rock and roll?" he asks as he opens the bathroom door. His long blond hair is neatly styled and his teeth shine in the hallway light.

"God, you're so white." We both laugh as we head out into the night.

COMFORT

There is stillness to my day. There is bliss. Calm is the mind that used to be chaotic. Quiet is the soul that used to yearn. A husband who took my last name, who makes me coffee every morning, the kitchen filling with the aroma of beans being ground. Soft, ever-white sheets. Sleep in my eyes. Fresh laundry with fabric softener and a dryer singing a happy tune when it's done. Gentle is the touch that used to burn. Mellow is the breeze that used to gust. Morning workouts at a fancy gym I can afford. Warm towels and cucumber water. Hot showers every day, sometimes more than once. Avocado ointment for puffy eyes afterward, coffee-infused cream for bright skin on my cheekbones. My morning pills, my morning protein shake in a crystal glass. Heavy is the pocket that once was empty. Steady is the hand that used to tremble. Bursts of writing in my office with floor-to-ceiling bookshelves and a special place for my Lambda Literary Award. A wallpapered accent wall on one side, and on the other a large mounted flat-screen TV, two video game consoles below. A collection of fridge magnets from the places I've visited: a tango dancer from Barcelona, a double-decker bus from London, an olive tree from Crete. Open are the borders that used to be locked. Endless are the trips that used to be denied. A friend who's a flight attendant.

A friend who writes YA novels with trans protagonists. A friend who travelled across the globe to join me here. A friend with red hair and a Cape Breton accent. A friend who texts how proud of me she is once a week. A friend who can't help but adopt yet another pet. They stood by us at our wedding, purple flowers in their hair, boutonnieres with Arabic poetry written on their leaves. Welcomed is the man who used to be an outsider. Loved is the man who used to be alone. Another event on the horizon. A closet lined with floral-print suits, traditional sherwal pants, and a red fez. Do you want to do a workshop on mentorship? Do you want to read from your debut novel? Do you want to write a children's book? Do you want to join a panel on trauma? Do you want to do a documentary? Do you want to write a memoir? Yes. Yes. Yes. Yes. Yes. I don't know.

My therapist says that self-monitoring and hypervigilance are classic symptoms of post-traumatic stress disorder. Writing a memoir, she explains, is dangerous business. High risk, high reward, I joke. She laughs. I laugh. I write a chapter. I get triggered so many times. I cry at night. Matthew holds me. My therapist tells me the worst is over. I feel better. I write some more.

I still wake up too early for my own good. A dark building with two lit windows looks like a monster crouching at the horizon. Mountains covered in fog. Rain in January and February and March. Rain in May and June and July. In Syria, we have a saying: "Impossible as rain in August." Not here. My skin goes weeks without seeing the sun. Pale is the boy who used to be golden. Cold are the fingers that used to pulse with heat. I forget Arabic words. What's mist in Arabic? What's nostalgia? I still get triggered sometimes—by the smile on a cute boy's face, the eyes of an intense actor on television, a fan holding a copy of my book and asking me to sign. I shiver, take a deep breath, and jump into one of my rehearsed lines to give myself enough time to find balance again, to find stillness. Strong is the boy who used to tremble.

I tell my therapist that the world has betrayed me many times before; why would I start to trust it? Why would I unclench my fist and offer it a hand? What's stopping me from deleting this whole document, forgoing this extended trust exercise? She tells me that I deserve better for myself. The world betrayed you, she says, and it's time to forgive it. Not because forgiveness is warranted, but because you're still standing. She explains that systemically the world wasn't made for people like me, but I still managed to fashion one that is—a small sliver of a world for me to occupy with lovers and friends. This forgiveness, she says, is meant to allow me to open up once again, to trust strangers with my history: the good and the bad and everything in between.

Do you think I should, dear reader? I've shared so much of myself. Is my history safe on your bookshelf? Are my stories compatible with your worldview or powerful enough to change it?

I'm choosing to sit here with comfort, trusting that they are.

ACKNOWLEDGMENTS

What is a memoir if not a long-form acknowledgment to all those who shaped me and all those who deserve my apologies. Still I would start by acknowledging my counsellor as well as my therapist, who took me in when I was weary, and without whom I wouldn't have been able to write this book from a place of power as I intended. Thank you to both.

Much love, today and always, to my mentor, John Vigna, for being my safe harbour; to my agent, Rachel Letofsky, for being my fearless advocate; and to my editor, David Ross, for being my watchful eye. The three of you, at various points in this journey, came to my aid when I needed it the most. I am thankful to have you—to push me, to care for me, and to celebrate me.

To all those who have supported my work at CookeMcDermid, and to the team at Penguin Canada, including Cameron Waller, Dan French, and Nicole Winstanley. It takes a village to publish a book, and I couldn't have picked a better village to settle in.

Thank you to Chris Morrissey, founder of Rainbow Refugee. Thank you for being part of my journey here to Canada and for all the lives you've saved, directly and indirectly, over so many years. You might not be a nun anymore, but you're a saint.

A million thank-yous to David Salter, who has been the healthiest father figure a man could ever hope for, as well as to Dara Parker, who nonchalantly saved my life, then became my friend.

I am thankful to the Writer in Residence program at the Haig-Brown House in Campbell River for hosting me as I wrote the first draft of this book. Special mention to my harbour on the island, Kyle Hilliard and Angelo Octaviano. Also to the University of Toronto Scarborough's School of Creative Writing for hosting me as I finished its final touches. I especially appreciate Andrew Westoll for the many conversations we had about this memoir.

Thank you to both the Canada Council of the Arts and the BC Arts Council for generously supporting me during the three years it took to write this book.

To those who agreed for their names to appear in this book, thank you. To my best man at my wedding, Cee Rouhana; to my first reader, Samantha MacDonald; and to my good Judy Bradley Babcock. To my best dude, Tash McAdam, and my Disney Gay™, Zac Brown. And a special woof to my dogs, Freddie and Dolly. You folks are my spirit family.

To those whose names I had to alter: Sama, Omar, Shiraz, Abdo, Ro, and all the others. The night might get dark, but you are my guiding stars. Thank you.

. . . and to you. Always to you. Home is an elusive concept for people like me, but you, Matthew Ramadan, will always be my home.

DANNY RAMADAN (he/him) is a Syrian-Canadian author, public speaker, and advocate for LGBTQ+ refugees. His debut novel, *The Clothesline Swing*, was longlisted for Canada Reads and named a Best Book of the Year by *The Globe and Mail* and *Toronto Star*. His second novel, *The Foghorn Echoes*, won the Lambda Literary Award for Gay Fiction and was shortlisted for the Ethel Wilson Fiction Prize and the Vancouver Book Award. He has an MFA in Creative Writing from UBC and currently lives in Vancouver with his husband.